THEIR EYES ON THE SKIES

by
MARTIN COLE

AVIATION BOOK COMPANY
Glendale   California

Copyright © 1979 by
MARTIN COLE

All rights reserved including the rights to
translate or reproduce this work or parts
thereof in any form or by any media.

LIBRARY OF CONGRESS CATALOG CARD NUMBER 78-74128

First Edition

Library of Congress Cataloging in Publication Data
Cole, Martin, 1904–
   Their Eyes on the Skies.
   1. Aeronautics—History.   I. Title.
TL15.C63   1979   629.13'0092'2 [B]   78-74128
ISBN 0-911721-09-6

For Ruth, who patiently waited.

Make No Little Plans. They Have No Magic To Stir Men's Souls.
        . . . Daniel H. Burnham

Foreword

During my long association with the American Aviation Historical Society there appeared in its *Journal* a series of articles by Martin Cole. Mainly, they dealt with personalities with vision and idealism. Also in common, the stories revolved around persons who had made great contributions without receiving proper recognition. I suppose much of the membership felt as I, that these stories were of the sort that should be read beyond the fold of the AAHS.

Now that certain selections are presented in THEIR EYES ON THE SKIES, aviation's heritage will be greatly enriched by it.

The stories range from the early flights of John Joseph Montgomery to the Cole Brothers, the last of the barnstormers. (Incidentally, author Cole is another of the Cole Brothers, and I note in the chapter he modestly refrains from saying so). In the early days Charles Willard contributed greatly to aviation's role, but sadly he has remained almost entirely unnoticed and unsung. On a personal note, I as a boy watched Charles Willard fly at the 1910 Dominguez Air Meet. His flights played a major role in germinating my early interest in aviation. Further stories concern Moye Stephens flying a Stearman on a world flight; Robert Short who died in China for an ideal; George Milligan's long career in saving lives and untold sufferings; and Nate Saint of the Missionary Aviation Fellowship who with fellow missionaries gave their lives for Christianity. Nate Saint and his wife Marjorie, whom I met at Shell Mera in 1946, were truly dedicated and quite fearless people. Aside from each pilot's superb flying skill that made possible adventurous achievements, all—symbolically speaking—had their eyes on the skies.

Someone once said the accurate recording of history is a task requiring great responsibility. Author Martin Cole is to be commended for bringing us certain overlooked sidelights of aviation's heritage. I'm sure the writings have been a pleasure because it has permitted him to meet that responsibility.

JAMES H. DOOLITTLE

Los Angeles 1978

Acknowledgments

When my stories first appeared in the *Journal*, published by the American Aviation Historical Society, it was understood by all concerned that later they might possibly be retold in a forthcoming book. In the preparation of THEIR EYES ON THE SKIES only seven of the original series were selected for inclusion. It was felt these offered most in keeping with the theme of the book's title.

The publication of the stories for the second time has given me the opportunity to add new information, correct several errors, revise the style and phraseology, and hopefully make each more lively, vivid and interesting.

In the preparation of these stories the many sources were documented and published in the *Journal.* Because certain individuals made worthy contributions, they deserve to be mentioned again. In order of chapter appearances they are: Rev. Arthur D. Spearman S.J., a foremost authority on John Joseph Montgomery—we worked together over a period of years to bring recognition to this forgotten pioneer; John Sloan, one-time editor of the *Journal*, together with AAHS director Herm Schreiner and myself, spent hours with the late Charles Willard making tape recordings of his early recollections; Moye Stephens permitted me to make use of his unpublished manuscript of the Stephens-Halliburton flight; Ed Short, brother of Robert Short, related eyewitness accounts of the air battle as told to him in China, and also arranged for the reading of his mother's lengthy manuscript; George Milligan supplemented newspaper accounts by telling of Mercy Flights trials and tribulations; Norman Olson permitted me to research the Missionary Aviation Fellowship files; and finally my long, close association with my brothers Duane, Lester and Marion who have held center stage for some thirty years in the world of aviation, made their story a must.

My thanks to the Bobbs-Merrill Company for permission to use quotes from *The Flying Carpet*, by Richard Halliburton. Also thanks to Duane Cole for permission to use quotes from *To A Pilot*, and *The Flying Coles*, both published by Ken Cook Company. I am most grateful for the attention editor Goro Suzuki of Tokyo, Japan, showed me by detouring his flight from Seattle to Japan by way of Los Angeles to discuss Robert Short with me. It is from his book, *New Frontiers in a Bold Sky* (this is a literal translation of the title), that I learned the Japanese viewpoint of the Robert Short air battles.

During the years I was editor of the *Journal*, we had on our staff a most capable art director. As a favor to me James Farmer has provided the art work for the book jacket and chapter headings. In addition to Jim Farmer's work, there is a line drawing of the 1883 Montgomery glider. For making it available I am grateful to Garland Goodwin. I am most grateful for the kind words written by Jimmy Doolittle in the Foreword.

This book probably would never have been written had not my wife, Ruth, encouraged me to give up the editor's job to devote full time to this and other books begging to be written.

MARTIN COLE

Whittier, California 1978

PHOTO ACKNOWLEDGEMENTS

- 8 (top) Martin Cole, (lower) A.D. Spearman.
- 14 (top) A.D. Spearman, (lower) Martin Cole.
- 23 Henry A. Liese.
- 40 U.S. Navy.
- 50 Moye Stephens.
- 66 Moye Stephens.
- 77 Edwin Short.
- 90 (top) The Boeing Company, (lower) Goro Suzuki.
- 95 George Milligan.
- 106 (top) Mercy Flights, Inc., (lower) Larry Holman via Mercy Flights, Inc.
- 116 (top) Kenn Knackstedt via Mercy Flights, Inc., (lower) Glunz Photo Service via Mercy Flights, Inc.
- 125 Missionary Aviation Fellowship.
- 140 (both) Missionary Aviation Fellowship.
- 154 (top) Lester Cole, (lower left) Duane Cole, (right) Marion Cole.
- 160 (top) Flying, (lower) Duane Cole.
- 163 (top) Martin Cole, (lower) Duane Cole.

Contents

The Several Flights of John Joseph Montgomery . 1

Charles Willard: Boy Wonder of the Air 19

The Flight to Never-Never Lands 43

The Making of a Hero. 71

Wings of Mercy 93

Nate Saint of God's Kingdom of Flying Men 121

A Hayfield for Takeoffs 143

Epilogue: A Message to the Boys of America 167

1

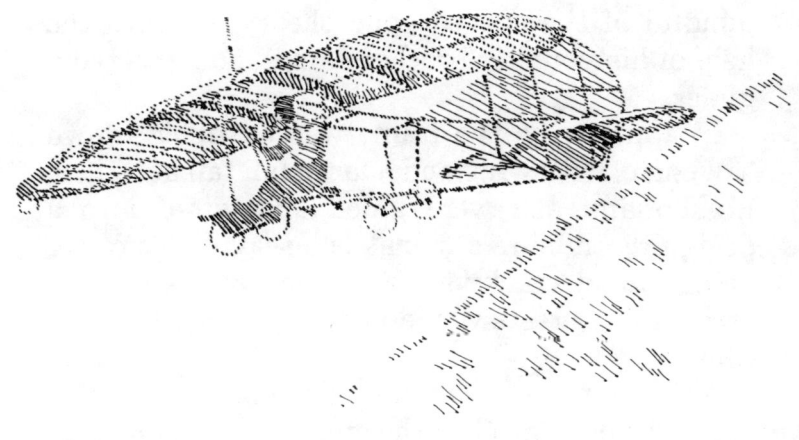

The Several Flights of John Joseph Montgomery

2 • THEIR EYES ON THE SKIES

The year is 1883. In the chronology of history the U.S. 7th Cavalry is chasing Indians on the western plains. The gasoline engine is yet to be invented. Kitty Hawk is 20 years away.

The concept of the curved wing—making possible sustained flight—is generally unknown.

But John Joseph Montgomery, a youthful farmboy living near San Diego, California, has managed to unlock the secrets of flight. He did so through serious investigations. Once he became mindful of the curved wing theory, he with the help of his younger brother James, constructed a glider.

In appearance the frame was an upside-down sawhorse, with wing and a large fan tail attached. Muslin and ash were glued and wired into a design resembling a monstrous seagull. To offset being called crackpots, the boys worked in secrecy. Flight tests would be made at nearby Otay Mesa.

And so it was that one morning, before daylight, the boys hitched the mules to a hayrack. On the hayrack, hidden under a covering of hay, was the glider. Before the neighbors had a chance to observe them, they were on their way to Otay Mesa.

When they reached the mesa, John pulled the team to a stop where the ground abruptly dropped off on a ten-degree slope. "This looks like the right sort of a spot," he commented.

Before them in the early morning sun was a

FLIGHTS OF JOHN JOSEPH MONTGOMERY • 3

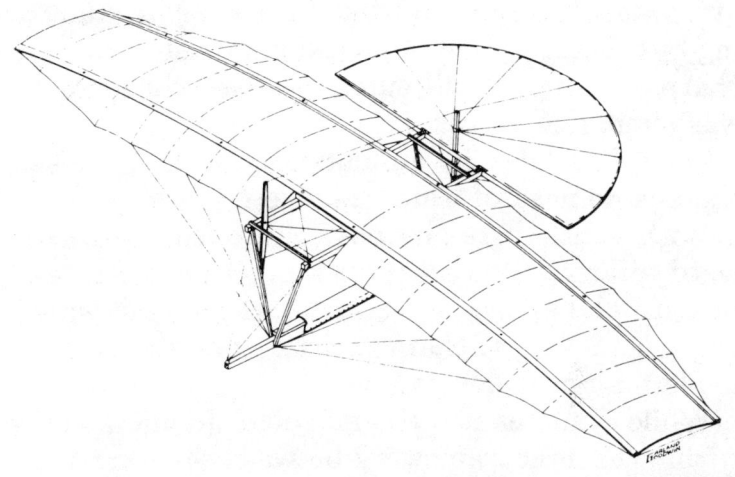

The Montgomery 1883 Glider
The Montgomery papers, James Montgomery's recollections, and other known data, made it possible for aeronautical engineer Garland Goodwin to prepare this drawing.

scene of pastoral tranquility. Beyond the slope, a mile or so farther, were the sparkling waters of the Pacific Ocean. And, off to the left, a short gallop away, were the sleepy huts of Tijuana on the Mexican side of the border.

After unhitching the mules the boys would await the strong offshore breezes that came during midmorning. So to kill time they first cooked breakfast over an open fire, and then engaged in target practice with the rifles they had brought. Occasionally John stood at the brow and tossed dirt to test the uplift of wind. Previously in studying bird flight he had observed gulls rising on the sharp deflection of air currents where the terrain was similar to this.

Sometime later he announced, "Well, I guess there is no need of waiting longer."

With gentle care the boys unloaded the awkward aircraft. The creation was as imperfect as modern planes are perfect. Still, the curved wing was one essential characteristic consistent with modern aircraft design.

While Jim steadied the machine, John crawled within the light framework between the wind and fan-shaped tail. In flight he would straddle a carpet-padded rail. His legs would hang down. Cautiously, the boys let the wind lift the 40 pounds of soaring machine until the padded seat was touching John lightly. The thermals on the 20-foot wing spread were causing some surging until John adjusted the big elevator, which has to be aviation's first stabilizer control.

Wind. Design. Pilot skill. Those were the factors invested in the flight. While John reflected on this, Jim tied a clothesline rope to the frame. That done, he stepped down the slope to the length of the rope. He took up the slack. He nodded and said, "I'm ready when you are."

This was it. The big moment. The moment John had in mind when he wrote his sister Margaret. "My attention is still fixed on my flying machine. ... At present I am making a large machine with which to test certain facts developed by a series of experiments carried on during the last few months. And I wish you always pray earnestly for my safety and success."

John Montgomery crouched for the spring.

"Ready ... set ... GO!"

What happened next is best told by James some years later when a successful lawyer.

"I pulled on the rope and then began running down the hill as fast as I could. Suddenly the rope went slack and I nearly fell. I looked back over my shoulder and there was John in the flying machine right above me.

"I was so excited that for a few seconds I just stood there. Then I began running after him, shouting as I ran. Through clumps of brush and around patches of cactus I went, my eyes on John and the machine.

"John was flying. The nearer he got to the ground the more he kicked his feet and swayed his body to keep balance. Towards the end of the flight he veered to the right to miss a clump of brush, and when he landed he came down so lightly he barely bent his knees."

Breathlessly the younger brother raced down the slope. He found John with eyes bright as he held the glider tugging in the wind. He exclaimed, "I had a glorious feeling of buoyancy!"

They talk and the high riding excitement spills over for another flight.

"Jim—I'm going to try and make it to the bottom of the hill this time."

They carried the glider up the slope. With high hopes Jim again pulled the launching rope at John's command. Again the flying machine became airborne. Then in shocked surprise the younger brother saw a wing dip. An instant later the machine flipped downward.

As John related later, "I was thrown headlong. As soon as I recovered I saw one side of the machine was smashed."

There is a legendary sequel to man's first flight. John was asked, "Now that you have flown, what good is it?"

Some years after the Otay Mesa flight, John, armed with a Master's degree from St. Ignatius College, San Francisco, began teaching Applied Sciences at Santa Clara College. Here his inventive mind, in quest of scientific development, led him into various fields. Among his patents were the telauloprint, a forerunner of the teletype; also, a gold separating machine. But more importantly he continued, with some interruptions, his investigations in aviation.

In 1893 Montgomery journeyed to Chicago, where he read a carefully prepared paper on his aeronautical findings before the Aeronautical Congress. He told of his early experiments, and for the first time related in public his flight at Otay Mesa. At this seminar he met Octave Chanute, the world-famous bridge designer, who was largely responsible for the correlation of aeronautic ideas. Chanute was impressed with Montgomery's pioneer findings. He offered to come west and work with Montgomery in designing aircraft. Montgomery, however, a loner at heart, advised Chanute of his true feelings—his preferring to work alone.

Models and full-sized gliders were turned out at the Santa Clara College workshop as Montgomery continued his search in the unknown. Then in 1897 he hit upon the idea of tandem wing gliders, a design he pursued intermittently for the next eight years. Finally, after much trial and error and hillside glider flights, Montgomery, with supreme confidence, announced an unprecedented public demonstration would be held on the college grounds. On April 29, 1905, he would demonstrate to the world a highly maneuverable craft, a pioneer development in its own right.

This time there would be no mere gliding off a hillside. To attest his theories of controlled flight, Montgomery wanted height, plenty of height. To gain this advantage he arranged to have the glider carried aloft by a balloon. Dan Maloney, a carnival parachutist, was engaged for the flight. To demonstrate complete controllability, Maloney would glide to a wheat field a half-mile away.

The announced exhibition attracted several thousand spectators. Included were reporters who would record the event for posterity. Not all of the onlookers gathered within the white-walled

8 • THEIR EYES ON THE SKIES

(Above) Where John Montgomery made man's first flight, a stainless-steel replica of a DC-3 wing commemorates the event.

(Below) Professor Montgomery during the Santa Clara years.

college grounds. Rather, many were perched on nearby roofs, or finding other places of vantage.

One must keep in mind this was an era when the Wright Brothers were either unheard of, or to some a preposterous myth. Thus it is understandable that the gist of the undercurrent comments was whether or not Montgomery was crazy to attempt what might well be the impossible.

There was an anxious wait as the balloon swelled pear-shaped to finally stand 40 feet tall. When all was ready Dan Maloney, dressed in red and white acrobatic tights, straddled the saddle within the framework between two single, tandem wings each with a wing spread of 24 feet. The wings, frail and drooping, with thin ribs and spars and an almost transparent silk covering, hardly inspired confidence. No wonder skepticism rode high among the bystanders.

In the final moments, Maloney once again tested the wing-warping foot stirrups and cords extending to the half-circle rudder. Satisfied, he called out, "I'm all set, Professor Montgomery. Let 'er GO!"

Montgomery, with a nod, released the windlass brake. The balloon shot upward.

In swift movement the strange configuration of balloon, glider and man soared higher and higher. It soared up to 1000 feet. Then on it went to 2000 feet. 3000 feet. 4000 feet. Now the balloon with its dangling glider was little more than a speck in the sky. The crowd remained hushed as they waited for the climax.

Would the descent be a successful downward flight?

Or, would there be a sickening fall ending in disaster?

Collectively they waited, each with his own thoughts, none hardly daring to breathe.

"There he goes!"

"He's falling—!"

"No, look—he's flying like a bird!"

And fly like a bird was the way reporters would express the event. At first the tandem wing glider spiraled downwards in graceful curves, but as Maloney got the feel of the machine he began experimenting. From the ground he could be seen swaying his body and using his arms and legs on the controls to not only fly in circles, but reverse direction and make dips that ended in upturns.

When it was evident that Maloney was gradually closing on the wheat field scores of excited persons by buggies, automobiles, bicycles, and on foot raced that way. One reporter who arrived as Maloney was touching down gives an eyewitness account.

"He soared like a bird over the center of the grain field, and swooped lightly to earth so gently that he did not even bend his knees. He stepped off the frail craft as a person might step off a bicycle. Cheers were given for him and cheers also for the inventor, who received many congratulations on the success of his machine."

Tidings of this remarkable first-flight-of-its-kind were telegraphed to newspapers across the country, and sent by cable to European papers. And so for the briefest moment John Joseph Montgomery captured headlines, but with no spectacular follow-ups to sustain his name, he was soon forgotten. Not until 1911 would his name be mentioned nationwide.

In the 28 years from 1883 to 1911 Montgomery's flying interest was never a continuous all-out pursuit as was with Orville and Wilbur Wright. All fields of science attracted him, and thoughts of financial independence spurred him at times to latch on to ideas that promised substantial gains. Some of the Montgomery inventions were moderately successful.

In 1911 a Montgomery improved glider (not tandem wing) was copied by Horace Wild, nephew of Captain Thomas Baldwin of dirigible fame. Wild installed a Bates air-cooled engine and reached speeds of 60 miles per hour. Mrs. Montgomery having observed how Bates had capitalized on a Montgomery design, urged her husband to give serious thought to developing—and marketing, of course—an improved wing design he had discussed with her. It must be presumed Montgomery needed no great urging. For sake of economy the testbed would be a glider. Field experiments would be made.

In the college workshop a high-wing, monoplane-type glider with an undercarriage of four baby buggy wheels took shape. There would be a sit-down seat and a butterfly control wheel. The ribs of the wing, as constructed by Joseph Vierra and Cornelius Reinhardt, were adjustable for curvature experiments. In the interest of making quick changes to various curvatures, the entire wing structure was bolted to the fuselage framework with 24 stovebolts. The ¼x3-inch bolts were longer than necessary and protruded in a hazardous way about Montgomery's head when he sat in the glider seat. Reinhardt insisted the unnecessary lengths be cut off, but Montgomery declined, saying, "No, we may need them as they are."

When all was ready, Montgomery and wife, Reinhardt and Vierra took tents, workbench and tools, along with the glider, to the Ramonda Ranch near the crossroads village of Evergreen. After making camp, the glider was assembled and taken to a preselected hill overlooking the valley. It had a hollow slope facing the direction of the prevailing northwest breezes. Short of the crest a runway ramp was built of wood troughs for the wheels to roll in during takeoff. During the preliminaries Reinhardt again worried about the protruding bolts. "Let me trim them off," he said, but Montgomery only shook his head and replied, "I may want to make some change that needs more length. Leave them as they are."

John Montgomery had a no-nonsense manner about him, even to his most intimate acquaintances. Characteristically, he plunged wholeheartedly into the trial-and-error experimentation. Because of the isolation, few witnessed the daily flights. Mostly those who came were neighbor children. The glider was occasionally modified in the workshop tent. At first it was not clear in the minds of Vierra and Reinhardt what Montgomery was attempting to accomplish, for in his close-mouth manner the Professor refrained from speculating aloud.

Perhaps one reason Montgomery remained taciturn was that his mind dwelt so far into the future that his beliefs were often considered downright idiotic.

"Someday aeroplanes will be flying through the air as numerous as birds," he is known to have said. (The credit for coining the word "aeroplane" goes to Montgomery.)

Flights and workshop changes continued as the days sped by. Each sunrise brought forth another day of hopeful promise. The length of the flights increased. Only a few were flown straightaway. Mostly they were broad turnarounds and landings as far up the hill as possible. The farther uphill the less carrying there would be. Of the some 55 flights made, Vierra flew almost as many as Montgomery.

With changes in wing design came changes in the controls. In haste, Montgomery, who was always impatient with time, abandoned the butterfly wheel and made use of a slipshod affair that bothered Reinhardt. To fly the glider the pilot

14 • THEIR EYES ON THE SKIES

(Above) Joseph Vierra flying at Evergreen with makeshift controls that replaced butterfly wheel.

(Below) Trailing edge of wing showing splice that resulted in sustained flight.

controlled certain phases of wing curvature and tail rudder with his feet, others with his hands raised to right and left above him, and one elevator control was by a strap around the waist attached to a stick behind the back.

The makeshift arrangement caused further arguments between Reinhardt and his boss. "I'm a master mechanic from Germany. Just tell me what is wanted in way of controls and I can make the changes," was the gist of his persuasions, and he generally added, "Let me cut off those extra bolt lengths."

But Montgomery was a stubborn man. The flights continued in a haphazard way.

At the end of 12 days, Montgomery's optimism was riding high. He was close to the ideal wing he perceived. He felt with one more day of flying he would prove his assumptions.

But first, there was a drastic change to be made in the wing design. The work began at sunrise. Four inches were clipped from the leading edge, and the trailing edge was greatly lengthened. This major change was time-consuming, and consequently there was no opportunity to improve the controls.

By midafternoon the wing modification was completed and the wing bolted to the framework with the same overlength bolts. The glider was carried to the top of the hill and placed on the runway ramp.

As usual there was the favorable offshore afternoon breeze to take off in. The glider, with Montgomery at the controls, after a short run down the ramp, lifted gracefully into the air. At the foot of the hill Regina watched from her tent. She saw her husband gain altitude, continuing higher, all the while soaring like a gull as he came and made a broad sweep above her and headed back on a reciprocal course. And she noticed he landed higher uphill than any previous flight. From below the hill it appeared to her he had made it back to the starting point.

Before the glider rolled to a stop, both Reinhardt and Vierra saw that Montgomery's face was wreathed in smiles. The expression told he was thrilled with the accomplishment. For the first time in aviation's short history, a glider had sustained flight on rising air thermals sufficiently to return to the starting position.

Cornelius Reinhardt rushed forward with a camera to record the happy smiles. The Professor waved him off.

"Wait until I make one more flight. I want to try something special."

Quickly the glider was placed on the ramp. Montgomery took his seat within the framework. Vierra gave the machine its sendoff push.

The glider shot down the runway and was immediately airborne. As it left the ramp it shot up sharply. From Reinhardt's position he could see the puzzled look that crossed Montgomery's face.

He saw Montgomery attempting to lean forward and raise himself in an effort to change the center of gravity. At about a 60-degree angle and less than 20 feet off the ground the glider stalled. It fell off with the right wing tip hitting first. Momentum flipped over the machine.

"What happened? Where am I?" the dazed Montgomery muttered as Reinhardt pulled him from the wreckage.

With Vierra's help they laid him on the grass. It was then discovered that a stovebolt had pierced the skull.

Regina, who had seen the accident, was hurrying up the hill when she met the two men carrying her unconscious husband down. She was grief-stricken. In their tent he was laid on a canvas cot. Vierra hastened to the Ramonda home where he telephoned Dr. J.I. Beatty of Santa Clara. The doctor in his haste took the wrong road. He did not arrive until two hours later. In the meantime Montgomery had died.

In summary it is rather sad that with Montgomery's gifted ability and selfless drive for accomplishment, that he should miss opportunities for greater fame. Mainly, his loss of fame (and fortune) was due to an uncompromising personality. With him there was that fixedness of purpose that both made and destroyed his life's pattern.

History has been unkind, for while ample credit is given to such pioneers as Lilienthal, Langley, the Wrights and Chanute, the credit to Montgomery has been by contrast rather meager. Some sources overlook the validity and even the historic reality of Montgomery's contributions. Actually, what has been mentioned in this brief article is but an iceberg tip of his lifetime investigations in electricity, mechanics, wireless communication, astronomy, and most notable of all—the conquest of air. Thus it would appear Montgomery is one of America's most bypassed historic personalities.

Fortunately, there is a reliable biography for the interested to turn to. After years of painstaking research, Arthur Dunning Spearman, S.J., of the University of Santa Clara, has compiled a definitive documentation. This 240-page book, well illustrated and annotated, entitled *John Joseph Montgomery; Father of Basic Flying,* may be purchased from the University of Santa Clara, Santa Clara, California.

2

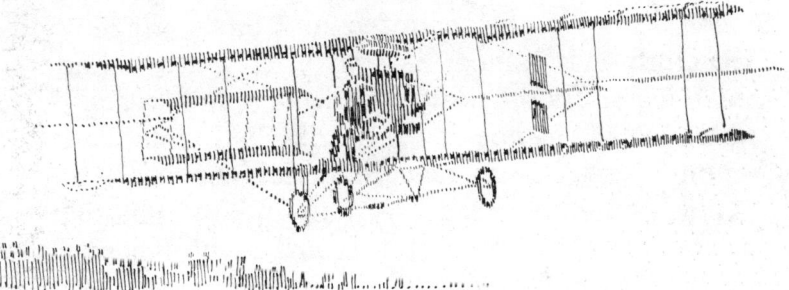

Charles Willard:
Boy Wonder
of the Air

"Don't go high. Keep her level. Landing is the important thing. Don't run into those people. And Charles, whatever you do, don't break it up."

Young Charles Willard, seated in the GOLDEN FLYER, nodded understandably.

Glenn Curtiss went on to advise little movement of the controls. "Just fly straight and level and land," he said.

It was a momentous occasion for Charles Willard on this early morning of August 3, 1909. Few persons in the world had flown an aeroplane. Those who had actually flown in Europe and America could be counted on one's fingers. Although man since the dawn of history had dreamed of flying, only in the last few years—moreover, in the last few months—had men flown beyond brief hops in powered machines.

Charles looked ahead. A half mile of pasture grass ended abruptly at a board fence where a small crowd had gathered. Near them were their parked automobiles. Stanley Steamers. Locomotives. Other high-wheelers of that day. Here at Hempstead Plains on fashionable Long Island some of the greatest wealth in America maintained estates. Charles had only to look out of the corner of his eye and see the elite crowding close to the GOLDEN FLYER. And looking closer he would have noted the restrained apprehension in their eyes. For in 1909, for a man to leave the earth in an aeroplane, was as great a step forward as man in modern times leaving earth for the moon.

CHARLES WILLARD: BOY WONDER OF THE AIR • 21

Charles grasped the control wheel. Settling himself in the aileron yoke he wet his lips and nodded. He was ready to add his name to the annals of aviation history. Curtiss flipped the propeller. The 22-horsepower Curtiss engine characteristically sputtered and popped before settling down to the rhythmic snorting of all four cylinders. The GOLDEN FLYER eased forward. Picked up speed. After a run of 200 feet it became airborne.

At an altitude of ten feet Charles leveled off. Amazingly he discovered no undue pressure was required on the controls. The GOLDEN FLYER handled beautifully. This was mainly because Curtiss had designed the aeroplane so that the center of gravity and the center of lift coincided.

Nearing the end of the half-mile flight, Charles allowed the GOLDEN FLYER to settle earthward. At one point he touched down momentarily. Easing back on the control wheel he lifted the aeroplane to finish the flight, barely skimming the grass. Keeping in mind Curtiss' admonition to avoid hitting people, he reached under the seat. His fingers touched and lifted the ignition switch. The GOLDEN FLYER touched down gently. To stop the rollout, Charles depressed a pedal with his right foot. The pedal activated a length of bamboo with a brake shoe just above the tire of the front wheel. Applied friction stopped the aeroplane.

There was at once great commotion among the spectators. They crowded about the GOLDEN FLYER. They poured out their congratulations.

Those sitting in the high-wheelers vigorously squeezed the rubber bulbs pumping air into the brass horns. The bulbhorns filled the air with an incessant squawking. Automobiles from the take-off area came hurrying up. Glenn Curtiss arrived.

The usually taciturn Curtiss was all smiles and congratulations. "Well done, Charles," he beamed. "It was better than my first flight."

For Charles such praise from Glenn Curtiss meant more than a handshake from the President of the United States.

The step by step of events that put Charles in the pilot's seat began a year previously in New York. At that time he had a promising career with the Gallagher-Winton automobile agency. Gallagher was a cousin of Stanley Yale Beach, the aeronautical editor of *Scientific American.*

In 1908-09 there was an awakening interest in flying machines. Throughout America hundreds of ideas were being built into contraptions that never got off the ground. Beach, with his knowledge of aeronautics, was willing to involve himself in a project. His relationship with Gallagher made him aware of a bright young chap working for his cousin. He knew of Charles being sent to France where he successfully licked the ignition problem plaguing the Rochet-Schneider automobile. The streak of genius of solving a problem baffling French engineers would characterize Charles throughout his life. Although still in his youth, he appeared, to older and sage minds, as one to bear

CHARLES WILLARD: BOY WONDER OF THE AIR • 23

The youthful Charles Willard seated in the *Golden Flyer* at Mineola, 1909. This aeroplane has been variously described as *Gold Bug* and *Golden Flier.*

watching. Charles was invited to join Beach in building a flying machine.

In those days the embryo aeroplane builder looked through various magazines for ideas. Charles had one advantage. The *Scientific American* library had up-to-date European publications. His perusal of them revealed they were far ahead of the American magazines in aeronautical information.

After a thorough study Charles concluded the big box affairs did not appeal to him. Nor would he consider the Bleriot type when he learned it was too sensitive for safe flying. In the end he went to Beach with a design based on the French Antoinette monoplane. The concept was agreed upon. Together they built the fuselage and empennage of what was to be known as the Beach-Willard. However, it never flew. Beach demolished it while taxiing without wings. With no brakes the machine ploughed through a board fence.

Beach's aviation interest led to establishing the Aeronautical Society of New York. In time arrangements were made to buy an aeroplane from Glenn Curtiss. The GOLDEN FLYER was bought for $5000. It was the first sale of an aeroplane in America. One stipulation of the sale was that Charles Willard be taught to fly.

Fired with the enthusiasm of making his first flight, Charles on the following morning was up with the sparrows. He would learn to fly in the still hours between daylight and when the sun was up a bit. When the air began to move around — he could tell by wetting a finger and holding it up — there would be no further flying.

Learning to fly would be self-taught. Curtiss had returned to his Hammondsport factory to build an identical aeroplane. This he would take to France to win honors at an international meet at Rheims.

During the first week the morning routine was a series of straight flights. Charles would fly the half-mile course, land, turn the machine around, and fly back. At week's end he began making timid flat turns and extending his flights. In the second week he was flying farther and farther.

The morning flights continued to attract a fair number of spectators willing to cut short a couple hours of sleep. One persistent sleep-loser was William K. Vanderbilt, Jr.

Vanderbilt, affectionately known as Willie K., was a multimillionaire playboy sportsman whose great love was auto racing. For five years he had sponsored the Vanderbilt Cup Races. It is said that rain or shine, he practically lived his waking hours in a 90 Mercedes racing car. So with thoughts steeped in competitive speed, with Charles extending his flights along a certain road, Willie K. one morning did not show up at the circus tent used as a hangar. Instead he parked the Mercedes where he anticipated meeting Charles on a return flight.

26 • THEIR EYES ON THE SKIES

Charles was not aware of a race in progress until he swung back on the country road and saw, 30 feet below, Willie K. hunched over the steering wheel of the speeding Mercedes. Now the GOLDEN FLYER had no throttle. It flew at one speed. Forty miles an hour. The Mercedes held the world record in speed.

Normally there would have been no worthwhile race. What equalized the situation was the condition of the road. It was narrow, rutted, and winding. Here and there were poorly graded culverts. Only a daredevil driver would use the road for a racecourse.

For two miles they seesawed. First one and then the other leading. The Mercedes kicking up a plume of dust occasionally scattered chickens strayed from a barnyard. When Charles swung aside to land, Willie K. slowed down. There was no real winner. But the race had a significance. It was the first contest between an aeroplane and automobile. In a few years hence, duels between pilots and racecar drivers would become a major attraction at county fairs.

Charles remained relatively unknown outside of Long Island until August 12. On that date, with only two hours of flight time, he upset the distance record.

On July 30, four days previous to Charles' solo, aviation had taken a giant step forward. Orville Wright, together with Lieutenant Benjamine Foulois in a Wright biplane, had set a distance record. They flew from Fort Meyer, Virginia, to a destination five miles away and returned. Advance publicity in the Washington, D.C., area accounted for a high state of interest. According to one newspaper prediction the flight would be "a grueling cross-country test." By takeoff time thousands had crossed the Potomac from Washington and were jamming the parade ground. Even the President of the United States, William Howard Taft, was there. For those who remained in Washington there was a downtown bulletin board to report whatever might be in progress—or conversely, possibly another fatal crash such as occurred six months earlier on that same parade ground. In the minds of everyone, the proposed flight was a feat hardly believed possible, yet deserving the highest plaudits if successful. When word was received of establishing the ten-mile record, "...the people of Washington went 'wild' over the news."

Now, 13 days after the "grueling cross-country test," a young upstart from the backwoods of Long Island would challenge the record.

The backwoods starting point was Mineola. Charles would fly an irregular course taking him over the rural towns of Garden City, Westbury, Hicksville, and a return to Mineola. The course would total 14 miles. The only advance publicity was by word of mouth, but it brought out some 400 well-wishers who saw him off at 5:26 A.M.

"I flew low, over wires, railroads and trees and

caused much excitement in that part of Long Island," Charles would recall.

Despite the early hour, the flight gave thousands of persons their first sight of an aeroplane. Skimming over farmyards and towns at 100 feet, Charles would see startled persons turn and look up. This was usually followed by gestures and the calling of attention to others to see the flying machine.

At Mineola the well-wishers with watches in hand calculated the return of the GOLDEN FLYER to be sometime after 20 minutes. When 15 minutes had passed, they, in anticipation, as one, faced east. Presently, a speck in the sky took on shape and grew larger. Then as they watched, the machine glided earthward.

With the goal only two miles away, the engine with no warning stopped.

"Suddenly I was faced with my first aerial dilemma—how to make an emergency landing."

But Charles had no need to be alarmed. Due to the GOLDEN FLYER'S remarkable design, with its perfect balance, he found himself gliding smoothly toward an open pasture in line of flight.

On landing the trouble was quickly determined. A wire had worked loose from the magneto. Charles had it replaced and was preparing to fly on to the starting place when cars began arriving. As soon as the drivers slammed on brakes, everyone piled out, climbed the fence, and raced across the field to congratulate the young flyer. He had set a new distance record. He had flown 12 miles. The event was a springboard to fame.

WRIGHTS' CROSS-COUNTRY FLIGHT BEATEN TWO MILES BY MINEOLA FLYER, was the generous *New York Times* headline. Newspapers across the country took notice.

Charles recognized the time was prudent to introduce the new-fangled flying machine to the public. He leased the GOLDEN FLYER. Within a few days after the record flight he was giving an exhibition at Athens, Pennsylvania. As America's first barnstormer he flew next at Richmond, Virginia. Then he appeared at Philadelphia before going to Toronto, Canada.

The Canadian National Exposition proved to be an unforgettable experience.

"You fellows are crazy. I can't fly out of here!" Charles was dumbstruck and rightly so.

When he arrived at the fairgrounds on the shore of Lake Ontario, he found his crew had set up the GOLDEN FLYER in a most impossible place. It was in the rear of administration homes bordering the lake.

"It's okay, boss," exclaimed a mechanic. "You can take off between the houses. You got three feet to spare."

Three feet to spare. Eighteen inches from an aileron tip to an immovable structure. "You guys are crazy to do this to me."

"It's the only place we could find, boss."

Charles met the situation in an ingenious way.

He built a wood trough that ran midway between the houses. The GOLDEN FLYER with its underbody skid riding in the trough would be guided accordingly.

Throughout the day while awaiting the calm air of evening, Charles had misgivings about the pending flight. There were only 50 feet of sandy beach beyond the houses. It would be the shortest takeoff he had ever made. With a small fortune riding on the flight, the risk was worth taking. Just to get off the ground and circle the fairgrounds would pay him more than the average worker made in a year. Came evening. Charles took his seat. The propeller was flipped. With the skid riding in the trough the GOLDEN FLYER cleared the houses. Charles had just gotten airborne when he reached the water's edge. So far so good. But—

Beyond the shore there was no horizon. A dense haze on the glassy lake gave no reference. Charles felt the front wheel touch water. Water splashed up. The wheel dug in further. The next instant the GOLDEN FLYER was standing on its nose in the shallow water.

It took three days to ready the GOLDEN FLYER for a second attempt. This time the flight over the fairgrounds was a successful crowd pleaser. However, on attempting to land he ran out of beachfront. Again he found himself in shallow water.

By year's end Charles had flown a series of exhibitions in the Midwest and Southern states. What

CHARLES WILLARD: BOY WONDER OF THE AIR • 31

was it like to be America's first barnstormer? Let Charles tell you as he reminisced those pioneering days.

"When I began flying there were no others in the exhibition business. The reason being the only flyable aeroplanes were Curtiss' and Wrights'. The Wrights were not available because the brothers were pursuing the military.

"My minimum fee was $1,000 and my contract stipulated fulfillment as long as I became airborne, whether it was for a minute or for an hour. My two-day rate was $1,500, three days $2,000, and for a ten-day meet it was $7,500.

"Traveling with me were a manager, mechanic and an ex-circus roustabout. We could always depend upon our circus man to pick a good drainage site for the tent, and once it was up it would stay up despite the hardest blow.

"We relied on the railroads for transportation, not only for ourselves but the aeroplane also. Nor did we ship the GOLDEN FLYER by slow-moving freight. Instead it went by express in the baggage car. You might say the express companies loved us."

The popularity of the international air meet at Rheims, France, prompted promoters in America to follow suit. Accordingly on January 10-20, 1910, Los Angeles was host to an event now known as Dominguez International Air Meet. On a plateau between Los Angeles and Long Beach, scene of a battle fought in the Mexican War, a grandstand was built to seat 25,000. Circus tents went up to serve as hangars. From the standpoint of attendance the air meet was a success. From 20,000 to 50,000 persons attended each day to see four aeroplanes make takeoffs and landings in open competition.

Those who participated were: Glenn Curtiss flying his Rheims machine. Charles Willard in GOLDEN FLYER. Louis Paulhan of France flying a Farman. Charles Hamilton, a Curtiss student, flying a No. 2 Curtiss.

Charles' boyish appearance endeared him to the crowd. One Los Angeles newspaper featured a cartoon by the well-known Herriman, showing the young aviator seated at the controls (mistakenly the controls were Wrights') with the caption: CHARLES FOSTER WILLARD; THE BOY WONDER OF THE AIR. The sobriquet became a sort of trademark that remained during Charles' barnstorming career.

The official program of Thursday, January 13, listed the cash prizes to be awarded that day. One listing in particular intrigued Charles.

> A PRIZE OF $250 WILL BE AWARDED TO ANY AEROPLANE WHICH STARTS FROM A RECTANGLE TWENTY FEET SQUARE, MAKING A CIRCUIT OF THE COURSE, AND LANDING IN THE SAME RECTANGLE.

After Charles told of his intention to try for the prize, workmen spread sawdust on a 20-foot-square area. When all was ready and the judges had taken their positions, Charles took his seat in the GOLDEN FLYER. His mechanic flipped the propeller. The flying machine rolled towards the sawdust marker. When the front wheel touched the sawdust, Charles eased back on the elevator control. The machine lifted. Now the trick was to circle and alight precisely within the square. When Charles made the circle and was seen approaching the area, everyone in the grandstand came to their feet. As he came in for a landing it was plain to see, at first, he was short. But Charles overcame the possible short landing by jockeying the power off and on. Skimming only a few feet above the ground he judged the proper moment to let momentum carry him forward. His judgment was good, for the wheels touched down and landed within the prescribed area.

As Charles alighted there was spontaneous clapping and cheering, and not a few ladies waved handkerchiefs. It was heady stuff for the young aeronaut.

It was during the air meet that Charles caused a phrase to be coined that was to plague the aviation world for some 30 years. Landing from a somewhat gusty flight, he was surrounded as usual by reporters eager for copy.

"How was the ride?" a reporter shot at him.
"Looked bumpy from here."
"Bumpy is right," Charles replied, and then with a grin made the off-hand comment, "The air was full of air pockets, as a Swiss cheese is full of holes."

"Air pockets" in the air caused Willard a bumpy ride, the reporter wrote in his column. The story was picked up nationwide. Before long pseudo-scientific articles were being written on the subject of "holes in the air." Thereafter, and especially during the 1920s and 30s, airplane crashes were generally attributed to "air pockets" and so were told in headlines. Not until about the time of World War II, when the press became knowledgeable, did the fable die.

Following Dominguez the months ahead were busy ones. Now flying a No. 2 Curtiss, Charles maintained barnstorming dates that had him crisscrossing the United States. He made aviation "firsts." For example, the first ground-to-aeroplane radiophone talk. The first experimental machine gun firing at a ground target. The first to fly in an aeroplane to be shot down.

History errs in telling us the first aeroplane to be shot down occurred in late July 1915, when Captain Hawker of the Royal Flying Corps did some accurate shooting with a carbine from his Bristol Scout at a German two-seater. Actually the date of the first aeroplane to be shot down was May 29, 1910. It happened at Joplin, Missouri.

Charles did not see the angry farmer aim his rifle and fire. However, witnesses did. The shot splintered the propeller. The immediate violent vibration would have torn the engine from its mount had not Charles cut the ignition. Fortunately he was in gliding distance of the exhibition field. When the farmer was arrested, Charles refused to press charges. He had learned in the meantime that ruthless spectators had knocked down the farmer's fence and trampled crops.

At least Charles Willard and Mark Twain had one thing in common. Both were to read of their deaths in the newspaper. One difference—Twain coined the immortal phrase of his death being "greatly exaggerated." Charles' forgotten exaggerated death occurred at Springfield, Missouri. While flying above a country club the crankshaft sheared off. The propeller flew back and chopped off a portion of the bamboo tail outriggers. The No. 2 Curtiss plummeted downward. Telephone wires broke the fall. Charles was thrown free, otherwise the weight of the engine would have killed him. As it was he hit the ground in a potato patch with such force that those who arrived believed him dead. A reporter believing him dead rushed to a phone to inform his paper. Moments later someone exclaimed, "He's alive. I saw his foot move."

From a hospital bed Charles read the newspaper account of his exaggerated death.

The tales of crowd misbehavior during the early flying days are sometimes difficult to believe. There are accounts of Lincoln Beachey and crew beating off angry crowds with clubs. Other flyers had similar experiences when mob psychology overrode pilots' instincts not to fly. It was at Oklahoma City that Charles was faced with intimidation and six-shooters. He flew against his better judgment.

It was at the State Fair Grounds on Friday, March 18, 1910, that Charles made the first flight in Oklahoma. He flew again on the following day. On both days the crowds were orderly. There was no reason to be otherwise. It was good flying weather. Sunday turned out to be different.

Despite the undersurface calm that prevailed on Friday and Saturday, the crowds were nevertheless made up of an entirely different fibre than what Charles was accustomed to. Three years previously Oklahoma was raw Indian territory. Those who came to the air meet represented the last vanguard of American frontiersmen. Oklahoma Territory was notoriously known as a refuge for hardcase characters. Undoubtedly it was this element that forced Charles to fly.

They tore down fences and surged into the infield. The officials were powerless to stop them. Their very numbers threatened to crush the No. 2 Curtiss. Charles knew he was up against it when he saw that some carried revolvers and all had been drinking heavily. A hardcase pushed his face close to Charles. He patted his holster. "You gonna fly or not?" he demanded.

Charles pointed to an anemometer. He tried to explain it was registering gusts up to 30 miles an hour.

"Listen bub, this Colt shoots 500 feet. Now if you know what's good for you—"

Charles did not take the threat of being shot too seriously. He did not discount the possibility, either. Definitely the more realistic threat was the destruction of the aeroplane. The crew was barely succeeding in preventing damage to the frail wings. The ugly mood was reaching a climax, fast. While the fate of No. 2 Curtiss hung in balance, Charles agreed to take a long, long chance and fly out.

He might have made it except for a deep gully in line of takeoff. Here the wind hit the near side and surged abruptly up. It was this updraft that caught the aeroplane. It slammed it nose-high into a stall position. Flying speed was lost. The machine hovered for a second or two, then dropped. Charles was badly shaken, but otherwise not hurt. The No. 2 Curtiss was a total writeoff.

The crowd had had their Roman holiday.

To safeguard against a crackup and lost exhibition dates, Charles had a Curtiss-type machine under construction. This was rushed to completion. During the summer a second machine was built with design improvements. Called the Express, it was powered with a 7-cylinder, 50-hp Gnome rotary engine. In performance it exceeded anything Charles had previously flown. However, the performance was insufficient for the 7,400-foot altitude of Mexico City.

Charles knew he was in trouble when the Express barely got off the ground. Failing to gain altitude he flew for a mile before daring to make a gentle turn. In the turn he lost altitude. To make matters worse he found himself over a corral of range cattle.

"I kept sinking until I was flying over their horns."

An adobe wall loomed ahead.

"I left the tail on the wall."

When the tail was repaired, Charles attempted to fulfill his exhibition promise. This time he failed to coax enough power to clear a field chopped up with shallow irrigation dikes. He hit the first dike. The second. The third— He lost count of how many there were. He kept hitting them until he was finally thrown from the seat. His foot caught and held in the undercarriage. Unable to free his foot he was dragged across plots. From one dike to another. On the Express went like a wounded bird, picking up speed between dikes but losing the gain at each obstruction. Somehow Charles was able to twist himself up enough to shut off the ignition.

As he lay beneath the machine with face bleeding from multiple cuts, a Mexican guard rode up. Hooking a leg over the pommel he began rolling a cigarette. When the first of the crowd reached the scene, the guard dismissed thoughts of giving aid by telling them, *"El gringo moriara."*

But scores of willing hands, ignoring the guard's prediction, lifted the machine off the gringo. And then the Samaritans did what they could to make Charles comfortable until an ambulance arrived.

It was fate, having much in store for Charles to fulfill, rather than a guard's dire pronouncement, that decreed death would be cheated.

One of Charles' achievements to be fulfilled was the development of an arresting gear making it possible for aircraft to land on ships. Charles was on hand during the January 1911 air meet in San Francisco when the U.S. Navy proposed a shore-to-ship landing. Two months earlier Eugene Ely had made the first flight from ship-to-shore. The event occurred at Hampton Roads, Virginia. After Ely flew from a wooden platform on the bow of the U.S.S. BIRMINGHAM there was an official urgency to accomplish a reverse flight.

The U.S.S. PENNSYLVANIA, a heavy cruiser, was conveniently anchored in the San Francisco harbor. A few miles away was the Tanforan race track where the air meet was being held. Ely was present with his Curtiss aeroplane.

A local newspaper publisher expressed an interest in sponsoring Charles for the shore-to-ship flight provided there was an assurance it could be accomplished. It was understood the Navy would build a landing platform over the gun deck. However, there would be insufficient length for an aeroplane's rollout. The unsolved problem was

40 • THEIR EYES ON THE SKIES

The flight that changed world history. Foreshadowing the role of the aircraft carrier, Eugene Ely makes successful landing on *USS Pennsylvania* with aid of arresting gear devised by Charles Willard.

therefore how to bring the aeroplane to a stop after landing.

"While the negotiations with the newspaper were pending, I immediately went to the Tanforan race track to develop the technology to facilitate the deck landing."

Here, without secrecy and in full view of the public, he began experimenting. Charles' Express was equipped with a "fail-safe" feature consisting of a rear-mounted, two-prong hook. It would dig into the ground when the control column was pushed forward all the way. Charles reasoned that somehow the hook must play an important role.

At first he considered a sharper hook to catch on the planks of the improvised deck. But this idea was rejected when his engineering sense told him it would not work. For if a hook engaged a plank slightly protruding, inertia would pull the aeroplane apart.

"Then the solution began taking the configuration of a series of rope barriers stretched across the path of landing."

To the ends of the ropes would be attached sandbags. In theory when the hook engaged the series of ropes, the sandbags would be dragged forward. There would be a consistent slowing action.

Although Charles developed the arresting gear, it was Ely in a Curtiss aeroplane that made the actual flight. Glenn Curtiss' close association with the Navy secured the historic honor.

The role of the aircraft carrier was foreshadowed when Ely made a successful landing using the Willard arresting gear. The Captain of the U.S.S. PENNSYLVANIA certainly recognized the significance. He declared, "This is the most important landing of a bird since the dove flew back to the Ark."

Over the years the arresting gear has been greatly refined, but in principle it remains essentially the same as when Charles developed the idea on the Tanforan race track.

In 1912 Charles hung up his exhibition goggles. He did so because he read the sign of the times. The lack of crowd attendance at the air meets was all too convincing. Whereas the Dominguez air meet drew crowds up to 50,000 a day, the succeeding air meets revealed that once people paid to see an aeroplane fly, and their curiosity had been satisfied, few would return again and again.

The infant aviation industry was showing promise of growing up. Charles perceived a need for engineering talent. He would grow with the industry. And he did. In a long span of years, his creative achievements covered a broad field of involvements that included, but was not limited to, aerodynamic design, pioneering in aero engine concepts, aircraft plant production and metallurgy. Although it has never been fully recognized, his most significant contribution must be regarded as the arresting gear that measurably influenced the course of world history.

3

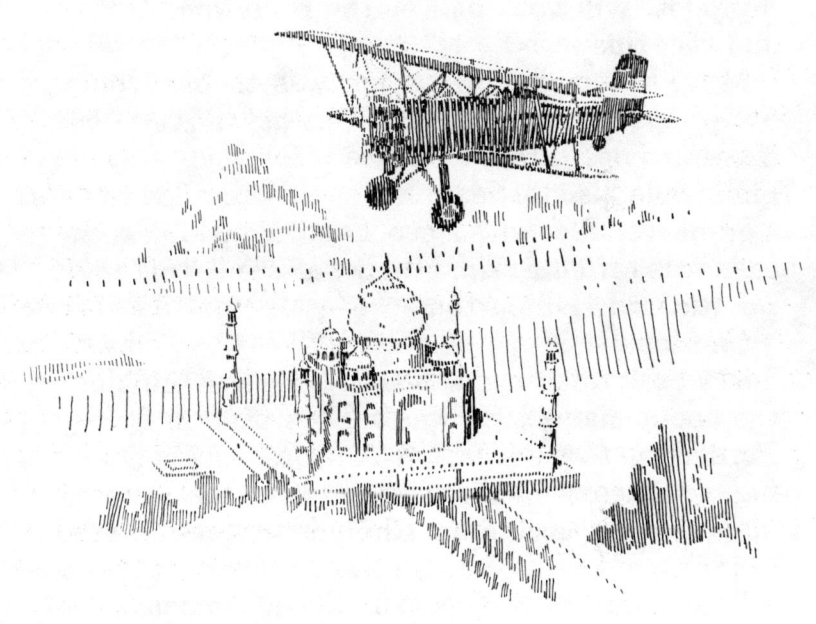

The Flight to Never-Never Lands

"I would like to speak to Mr. Moye Stephens."

"This is he speaking."

"I am Richard Halliburton." For a second or two there was a lifeless vacancy on the phone line. Then the voice continued. "Mr. Stephens, I am going to fly around the world. I want you to be my pilot. Will you come to the Hollywood Hotel and talk this over?"

Moye's immediate reaction was to blurt out, *Sorry, but President Hoover has asked me to be Secretary of State*. But a wee inner voice stayed him, while his startled mind swiftly recalled that a prankster pilot with a penchant for making such calls was off on a trip. Maybe, after all, this was *the* Richard Halliburton.

Cautiously, Moye answered, "Why . . . why I guess I can talk to you about it." He was thinking too about his job. He was a TWA captain flying Ford Trimotors out of Los Angeles. Likely nothing would come of the meeting other than an opportunity to meet Richard Halliburton. "I have tomorrow free—"

"Splendid. How about in the afternoon, say around two-thirty?"

"Two-thirty. That will be fine."

"See you then. Good-bye."

"Good-bye."

In the year of 1930, when this conversation took place, America had its many favorites. Looming high on the list of those idolized, yet today practically forgotten, were such names as

Gary Cooper of the movies, Babe Ruth of baseball, and Richard Halliburton, whose books stirred romantic dreams in the hearts of millions.

It all began with *The Royal Road to Romance*, a story of Richard's two years as a penniless world traveler. It was a *different* book. Different in that the young author unburdened his heart in fanciful reliving of history, myths and legends. Likely no other person ever enjoyed his kind of life to the fullest. While most everyone has romantic dreams, and a few make some come true, Richard's, in contrast, was a whole life exemplified in one never-ending romance. He had the capacity to see, and make others see, the marvels of forgotten worlds. For him the past was not dead, but filled with eternal heros. *The Royal Road to Romance* was an immediate international best seller, to be translated and read in Denmark, Holland, Sweden, Norway, Germany, Hungary, Italy, France and Czechoslovakia.

Two equally successful books followed. They were *The Glorious Adventure*, and *New Worlds to Conquer*.

For five years Richard had been riding the crest of popularity. American fans mobbed him in bookstores. Autograph seekers invaded hotels where he put up. Mail poured in by sackfuls. In 1930 the message was still clear. Travel and write.

Travel and write. But where to? Hadn't he done everything?

No, not quite. This was pointed out to him in

Hollywood where he had come to sell movie rights.

"Buy an airplane. There's plenty of places no airplane has gone," suggested a former RAF pilot.

The idea of aerial vagabondage intrigued Richard. He would buy a plane. His thoughts soared in fancy. He would name his plane THE FLYING CARPET. He would fly to Timbuktu. To Samarkand. Over the Taj Mahal. In short, he would go wherever capricious sirens beckoned. Not being able to fly, he would engage a pilot for the venture.

Richard shrewdly realized the success of a world flight depended much on whom he selected. Help came from the Department of Commerce. They suggested he get in touch with Moye Stephens. It was pointed out Moye came from an old California family and was a graduate of Stanford University. Moreover, he had been flying since he was 17 years old. Although he was only 24, he was an airline captain.

And that was how Moye came to get a telephone call and heard the other say, "I am Richard Halliburton ... Mr. Stephens, I am going to fly around the world. I want you to be my pilot. Will you come to the Hollywood Hotel and talk this over?"

Moye Stephens' unpublished account of the world flight relates in part their first meeting.

"My first impression of Halliburton was one of surprise at his slight build and medium height of the boyish handsome, vibrant young man that greeted me.

"The graciousness of his reception put me at ease at once, and his apparent absorption in my every word was most flattering. It was a characteristic which lent much to his persuasiveness. The effect was heightened by his trait of tilting his head slightly to one side while listening with seemingly undivided attention, at the same time regarding the speaker intently with ingenuous blue eyes. His darkish blond hair held the suggestion of a redheaded forebearer.

"Not surprisingly, Halliburton was a superlative talker and in a cultivated voice containing no trace of his southern origin, he recounted the events leading to the phone call."

Richard's book, *The Flying Carpet*,* makes generous use of poetic license to tell of this meeting.

> "The moment we met, I was impressed by his self-possessed appearance and quite capable manner; so I came straight to the point.
>
> "Stephens, I've just given myself an airplane. I want to fly it to all the outlandish places on earth. Will you be the Captain?"
>
> "Certainly. I'll go."
>
> "All right—we're leaving in half an hour."
>
> "I can't do that—not in half an hour. There's the transport company. My plane and passengers."

*The Bobbs-Merrill Company, 1932.

"Oh, resign! Your plane is only a big passenger bus anyway. I tell you I've got a flying carpet."

"Guess I can fly carpets, too. But where are we going?"

"We're going to Turkey and Pasadena and Persia and Jerusalem and the North Pole and—Paris," I said, leading him out the front door. "We're going to fly across deserts and over mountains and rescue imprisoned princesses and fight dragons"—pushing him into a taxicab.

"Well, for heaven's sake," he remonstrated, "—wait till I get my hat, will you!"

Actually weeks of preparation followed this meeting. Moye arranged for a year's leave of absence from TWA, although Richard was certain the leisurely world trip would take nearly two years. For one making $80,000 a year in books and lectures, the financial part of the trip was assured.

"We must have a thoroughly reliable plane and engine capable of getting in and out of tight fields," Moye advised. "It's got to be rugged enough to take a lot of wear and tear. There's only one plane I would recommend."

Richard waved his hand in a gesture of dismissing costs. "Just name it," he said.

"I figure a Stearman two-place, open cockpit biplane with a Wright-Whirlwind J5 engine will give us a reasonable chance of success."

A used plane dealer found the plane and engine Moye was seeking. A firm building an experimental Apache engine had purchased a Model C3B Stearman for its testbed. When the Apache engine failed to meet expected standards, the unflown Stearman was put up for sale. Concurrently, another firm building an experimental plane of substantial size had purchased a 220-hp Wright-Whirlwind. When the test flights proved the engine to be inadequate, it was put up for sale. It was the mating of this Stearman and engine that made up THE FLYING CARPET.

Modifications were made of the Stearman. Oversized wheels replaced the regular ones. Two eight-and-a-half-gallon gasoline tanks were installed outboard the main wing tank of 40 gallons. These, with a 20-gallon tank in the fuselage, gave a cruising range of 700 miles in eight hours' flying time. While the modifications were the decision of Moye, the scheme of colors for the new paint job was Richard's. He ordered the fuselage painted a brilliant scarlet with the words in black, THE FLYING CARPET, on a gold stripe that ran along each side. The cowling and struts were a shining black. The wings were pure gold—so they appeared when flashing in the sun. When all was ready the Stearman was flown to New York, where it was put aboard a steamship bound for London.

The book, *The Flying Carpet*, takes the reader directly to Timbuktu, deep in Africa, and reached from Europe by crossing the Sahara desert. The French authorities in Morocco regarded Moye and Richard as madmen to attempt a flight across this million square miles of lifeless sand, too arid to sustain insects. For 1,300 miles, from the

Richard Halliburton (left) and Moye Stephens were carefree vagabonds that saw a complacent world during the Golden Era of Romance.

French Foreign Legion post at Colomb Bechar to the Niger River on the southern end of the Sahara, they must keep in sight dim, windswept ruts of a seldom-used truck route. Early in the flight they could refuel at the tiny oasis of Adrar, but thereafter they would be flying over an infinity of cinderburnt sand as merciless as the moon. Somewhere along the route, they must spot a lone gasoline pump, land and refuel. Only once had the French military attempted such a flight. It had ended in disaster. The pilot and observer failed to see the pump, flew on until they ran out of gas. Later, when found, the bodies lay close to the downed plane, tragic victims of thirst.

"*Suivez la piste toujours* (Follow the track always)," was a French officer's advice.

When all was ready—with gasoline tanks topped off, with two weeks' supply of food and water aboard—the heavily laden FLYING CARPET took off in the morning's hot, dry air. It rose slowly, an inch at a time . . . turned . . . and faced the Sahara.

New York to Chicago. That was the comparative distance. Moye must keep his eyes glued to a thin thread of ruts and hold to course. But keeping the *piste* in sight could not be accomplished by forward visibility from the cockpit. Only by draping his head outside the windshield and peering down was he able to observe the lifeline. This meant his face was continually blasted by the slipstream of superheated air. This, too, he would have to breathe. Yet there was no other way of piloting if he were to *"suivez la piste toujours."*

As THE FLYING CARPET began a long, steady climb, so did the sun creep upwards. With each passing mile the sky became more and more dazzling bright. The hard, flat, ash-yellow surface of the limitless Sahara, broken only by faint wheel tracks, threw back the sun's glare and the heat that was generated. Moye and Richard had been warned that the Sahara would be an inferno. Normal temperature generally ranged well above 120 degrees, with as high as 175 degrees having been measured. At 5,000 feet Stephens leveled off. The wheel tracks were faintly discernible and surprisingly did not always continue in a direct line. Thus to lose sight of them meant they might not be found by holding to the same course.

The heat and sun became a torment to be endured. The horizon, Moye noted, was fuzzed with shimmering heat. And then it happened.

Suddenly, as if by some magic persuasion, the tracks vanished. Looking rearward, Moye saw with relief, the back tracks were still in sight. Keeping them in sight he flew at reduced throttle and nearer the ground, the lost *piste* became faintly visible, and then more so.

The hours and miles rolled by with Moye's eyes strained to keep the wisp of tracks in sight. Time and again he lost them, flew lower or wheeled about to pick them up—lost them—found them—playing a life-or-death game of hide-and-seek.

But Moye was forced to meet the ultimate skill of piloting when the tracks for a hundred miles or more were practically obliterated. As the lifeline gradually faded, so did Moye bring the plane lower to keep it in sight. At 50 feet when the tracks were becoming less and less visible, Richard, who was riding in the front cockpit, turned and gave Moye an inquiring look.

"I got to get lower," Moye yelled.

At 20 feet the tracks continued to fade. Also at 10 feet. And then Moye let down until the wheels of THE FLYING CARPET were inches above the hard, flat desert. Flying at 90 miles per hour, he could, by the most intent concentration, pick up what remained of the wind-washed, sand-filled tracks 50 feet ahead. With only a minimum of dihedral in the wings, THE FLYING CARPET was not a "hands off" airplane to fly, so for an hour or so it took delicate and sensitive handling. And during this long ordeal Moye never dared take his eyes off the tracks, never once got a moment of relief from the cramped flying position, and all the while he endured the fiery blast of the slipstream.

But when this crisis was past, when the *piste* was once more reasonably visible, there came the making of another crisis.

Moye had estimated the flight time from the refueling stop at Adrar to the life-giving pump to be three and three-quarter hours. It was an estimate based on a no-wind condition. With the desert offering no check points to determine ground speed, the wind factor would remain unknown.

A possibility of a tail wind made it necessary to be alert earlier than otherwise. Moye and Richard fixed their eyes on the trail for a pump that might appear from the air indistinguishable from the sand in color. When the fourth hour passed, fifteen minutes beyond the estimated arrival, apprehension grew with each passing minute. Had they overflown the pump as did the French flyers?

A half hour passed. By now each was seeing ghost pumps.

Forty-five minutes overdue—. Moye saw the anxiety written on Richard's face and could only guess as to his own.

And then Moye spotted several gasoline cans. It was a possible clue.

He made a hasty landing, and there at closeup was the pump, sandblasted beyond color recognition by a thousand winds.

Later Moye's sentiments were expressed by Richard who wrote, "A thousand eyes would never have seen it from above."

The headwinds that had delayed them en route later forced them to spend a most discomforting night on the desert. The temperature dropped 75 degrees. Moye's lungs seemed on fire, breathing was painful, nevertheless he and Richard endured a shivering night.

"You have burned your lungs. It will go away," a French doctor told him on reaching Timbuktu,

THE FLIGHT TO NEVER-NEVER LANDS • 55

and indeed it did. After a few days the burning sensation passed away.

The legendary Timbuktu, with Richard's visit, was to become known to millions of readers not as a fanciful name, but as a dying, stork-infested city that in its thousand years of history was once glorious. Being in an isolated corner of the world was a new experience for Moye, and during their stay the thoughts of the return trip occupied his mind. But the return trip proved to be uneventful, mainly because a motor caravan in the meantime had renewed the tracks.

Before leaving Africa, Moye was to have one more experience bordering on disaster. Popular stories of the French Foreign Legion fighting to the last cartridge suggested to Richard that he gather copy, so several weeks were spent in various military posts. They had arrived at one outpost deep in Arab land only a day or so after a savage attack had been repulsed at the very walls of the fort.

During the noon-hour siesta Moye, believing all danger was past, left the compound in search of guns and shells. He strolled the sand dunes without the protection of a firearm. Prior to leaving the United States he and Richard had purchased revolvers. These were impounded by French customs. Thus among the sand dunes he was without a means of blowing out his brains if captured. In that hostile land instant death was preferred to the heinous torture of the Arab women. What Moye was not aware of was that there were still Arabs lingering in the area. Fortunately before he had gotten far he was spotted by a sentry. In excited French he aroused the garrison.

In a manner somewhat like a Hollywood version of the 7th U.S. Cavalry come to the rescue, so did the legionnaires come charging.

"*Mon Dieu,*" exclaimed the lieutenant when all was safe within the fort, "if you had been captured, your body would have been thrown over the wall—" He paused for emphasis, then gestured as Frenchmen will, "in *petit* pieces."

Back in Europe, Richard locked himself in a Paris hotel room to write the African stories. When his work reached satisfaction, he spread the map of Europe and chose the Alps. What he really wanted was to visit the Matterhorn, scene of his very first conquest. And this he did with Moye piloting THE FLYING CARPET above the peak. The Matterhorn had not changed so much as a stone in the intervening years, nor had Richard's philosophy for living. That he should revisit the mountain in an airplane of his own, on a world aerial vagabondage, assured him that he had not begun to fossilize. Speeding over the Alps and into Switzerland, he reminded Moye that high on his want list was a desire to ride an elephant over the Alps into Italy, to emulate Hannibal's campaign against the Romans. Someday, he told Moye, he

THE FLIGHT TO NEVER-NEVER LANDS • 57

would come back and make that elephant ride.*

The Holy Land attracted Richard next. Here he and Moye remained for two months probing the inexhaustible subject of Bible history. As a consequence, familiar and fascinating Biblical stories were woven into the narrative of their stay.

Heliopolis is a Greek word meaning "sun city." Heliopolis, Egypt, is located near Cairo, and in the 1930s was a base for the Royal Air Force. It was here the modern Icarus who had tempted fate many times came close to terminating his adventurous career.

Richard had often said he would not die in bed. Someday, somewhere, he expected death to come under dramatic circumstances. He had cheated death in several instances. Each time, however, he lived to tell the tale, thanks to no one but himself.

The near tragedy occurred during an air meet. Normally when a pilot wishes to give his best performance no passenger accompanies him. But this time Moye made an exception when Richard asked to fly through the maneuvers.

In the holding area, just off the end of the runway, Moye ran up the engine. After testing the magneto drops, he tapped Richard on the shoulder.

"Seat belt tight?" On a few occasions he had

---

*Halliburton returned in 1934 and astonished—and amused—the world with just such an elephant ride. The story appeared in *Seven League Boots*. Bobbs-Merrill Company, 1935.

discovered Richard's failure to fasten his safety belt.

Richard made a quick check and gave an okay nod. Moye wheeled the Stearman onto the runway and took off in a climbing turn. On coming around he began a low pass and a slow roll for openers.

The plane was approaching a knife-edge position when Moye saw with gut-wrenching horror that Richard was slipping out of the cockpit.

All of his body from knees up was out of the cockpit.

Richard was flailing his arms in an attempt to grasp a handhold.

With a mind registering the scene like a stuck motion picture frame on the screen, Moye reacted instinctively.

He reversed the controls.

What saved Richard was two things. The reversing of the roll and Richard managing to grasp a handhold.

Back on the ground the cause was determined. When Richard fastened the safety belt he had not taken up the slack from the loop he was sitting on.

Petra. Bagdad. Teheran. Eastward was at a leisurely pace. One must read *The Flying Carpet* to find the rich meaning of ancient history as Richard saw it. In Bagdad and in Teheran Richard was royally entertained. In fact, wherever he went—in Europe and elsewhere—he was pulled into the ranking social orbit. Cocktail

THE FLIGHT TO NEVER-NEVER LANDS • 59

parties. Formal dinners. Embassy lawn luncheons. His books were now translated into 18 languages. Consequently among the literate populace he was as well known on the other side of the earth as on Main Street, U.S.A. Always when invited, Richard made it plain that any invitation for himself included his flying partner. Although their baggage was limited to essentials, dinner jackets were a must.

After flying the Sahara, the deserts of Arabia and Persia held no terrors, except a possible forced landing among hostile Arabs. They flew without escort, although they were aware of how R.A.F. planes flying the same route had at times flown cover for a downed aircraft until the pilot was rescued. The revolvers impounded by the French were never returned. So Moye provided himself with a Colt Super .38 automatic. He carried it in a shoulder holster under his flight jacket. It was never mentioned to customs officials. Fortunately, he never had occasion to use it.

From Bushire on the Persian Gulf to Karachi, India, was 1200 miles over the route Alexander the Great traveled on his return home after conquering India. The two-day desolate coastline flight was enlightened with Elly Beinhorn of Germany flying alongside in a Klemm sport plane. She had met them in Bushire. It was while Moye was servicing the Stearman that a desert-weary Ford approached. Much to his surprise a very attractive girl in her early twenties climbed out.

"Had a motor failure and a forced landing—hundred kilometers up the coast," she said. "I'm looking for a mechanic to help me make repairs."

"There's no mechanic here—except me," said Moye, "—but I'll do what I can. I'm an American pilot flying to India with Richard Halliburton. My name is Moye Stephens."

She flew with Moye in THE FLYING CARPET to her downed plane. He soon located the trouble and corrected it. At Bushire she and Moye and Richard formed a flying club with Elly president. Her duties were to patch Moye's threadbare pants and give each a haircut with a nail scissors.

From Karachi Elly accompanied them to the famed Taj Mahal, making the 800-mile flight in one day and arriving on Christmas Eve. Above the domes and minarets of the Taj, Moye did a slow roll as a salute to Emperor Shah Jehan for his great love for his beloved wife, Arjemand.

Richard, in search of further copy, turned his attentions to Mount Everest. In 1931 the 29,141-foot glacial summit had not been conquered by man or airplane. This was largely due to Nepal's rigid isolation. In those recent years the Nepalese government had refused adventurers an access to the forbidding slopes of the Himalayas, a fact that did not dim Richard's optimism. Even after his formal application was rejected, he continued to rely on his adeptness of finding ways to do the impossible. Opportunity

THE FLIGHT TO NEVER-NEVER LANDS • 61

came when Moye and Elly were invited to participate in an airmeet at Calcutta. The airmeet was arranged for the Maharajah of Nepal who was visiting there. The 80-year-old ruler with a long, flowing Santa Claus beard had never seen an airplane. His royal tent was pitched close to the runway.

Calcutta had never seen such aerobatics as Moye and Elly performed. At the very first power dive, the Maharajah was on his feet. Throughout the aerial maneuvers he was as excited as a small boy. He was amazed at the astonishing things people were doing outside his hermit province. For Richard it was a timely moment. He made Elly his spokesman. Through an interpreter she asked permission for them to fly to Mount Everest. A photo taken at this propitious moment shows the winsome flying fraulein standing before the bearded ruler. The twinkle in his eyes tells all too plainly he is completely captivated by her femininity.

Moye and Richard hardly dared breathe while waiting for an answer. But, thanks to Elly, the permission was granted.

Beyond Siliguri on the Nepal border, the Himalayas rise abruptly—and continue rising to form a vast chain of some 150 jagged peaks, each over 24,000 feet high. Beyond Siliguri there was no known spot where a plane could land. It was decided after the two planes arrived at Siliguri to go by car to Darjeeling where, from a distance of

125 miles, Moye and Richard could attempt a study of the bewildering panorama of snowy peaks and fix a course to fly.

Elly's Klemm, with a top ceiling of only 12,000 feet, would make no attempt to approach Everest, for within a few miles of Siliguri the mountains were actually that high. It was hoped THE FLYING CARPET, with a ceiling of 18,000 feet, could at least get within twenty miles of Mount Everest.

On returning to Siliguri a strange sight greeted the trio. There in the meadow where the planes were tied down, there, ringed about the machines, sitting tightly together, were hundreds of natives. They had never seen a plane, moreover they were totally unaware that airplanes existed. In their minds the planes were some sort of big birds; for after all only birds could fly. And they had seen the big birds land, and seen them tied down. But birds of that size surely could break the flimsy ropes, they reasoned, so patiently they had waited while Moye, Richard and Elly were in Darjeeling, believing sooner or later the big birds would tire of waiting and break their ropes and fly away.

In the cold, wintry dawn, Moye and Richard took off with THE FLYING CARPET stripped of every surplus ounce. It was January 9, 1932, Richard's thirty-second birthday. Elly accompanied the pair as far as Darjeeling, then with a wave turned back. The cold penetrated beneath their fur-lined flying suits as they reached 15,000 feet. For an

THE FLIGHT TO NEVER-NEVER LANDS • 63

hour they paralleled the Himalayas west of Darjeeling, then turned north to fly toward Everest some 70 miles away. Higher and higher each succeeding ridge reached toward them while the Stearman labored in thin air. Stephens pushed the plane up to 17,000 feet, and still the ridges pursued them.

With the rpm's into the tachometer's red-line area, the Stearman flying in a nose-high position made it slowly, ever so slowly, up to 18,000 feet. The icy slopes were barely 500 feet beneath. Fifteen miles from Everest—identified by the wind-driven plume of snow off the summit, THE FLYING CARPET had reached the absolute ceiling.

Richard was moved by the closeup view. "... indescribably magnificent, taunting the heavens ... this Goddess Mother of all mountains!" he would write.

The straining Wright-Whirlwind J5 was pushed to the limit. The Stearman vibrating with loose controls was on the verge of stalling.

It was while hanging short of a stall that Richard stood up.

He stood up to photograph Everest.

The added drag tipped the aerodynamic scales.

Down plummeted the Stearman.

Down it went on a crash course with rocks and snow. There was small chance of survival.

But Moye, the super pilot he was, reacted instantly. He shoved the stick forward—all the way. Only by a steep dive would he succeed in gaining needed wing lift. For milliseconds it appeared they would not make it. But moments short of their deaths, he maneuvered the Stearman into a downhill run.

It took five miles of downhill run before Moye considered it safe for his passenger to stand and photograph Everest. Even so at the lesser altitude the plane was still vibrating sufficiently to blur the picture somewhat. Nevertheless, although lacking in quality, it was the first aerial picture ever made of Everest, and importantly, it offered proof for one terribly sensitive to his critics.*

Calcutta. Rangoon. Bangkok. Singapore.

Without adequate charts, without weather information, Moye flying "by guess and by gosh" led the way with Elly trailing from Calcutta to Rangoon to Bangkok. The last day's flight into Bangkok was over 400 miles of impenetrable jungle. They could not so much as see the ground. Richard wrote his parents, "I think I was more nervous over that stretch than over any place we had flown, but the engine functioned perfectly, and we reached Bangkok on schedule. Moye continues to be the world's best pilot. Once in the air, no matter where, everything goes like clockwork." **

---

*Not until 1942 was Mount Everest conquered by air. Colonel Robert Scott, flying a P-43A equipped with turbo supercharger, circled the summit at 40,000 feet. The story is told in Scott's *God Is My Copilot*. Charles Scribners Sons, 1944.

***Richard Halliburton: His Story of His Life's Adventures*. Bobbs-Merrill, 1940.

THE FLIGHT TO NEVER-NEVER LANDS • 65

Elly, intrigued by the marvels of Siam, delayed her flight to Singapore. The Americans went on alone. Later she would fly on to Australia.

In Singapore THE FLYING CARPET was fitted with pontoons. Before leaving the United States Richard had purchased a set built for a Fairchild 71-A. These were shipped to Singapore. He also made arrangements with the Stearman factory to build struts, and although they agreed to, they failed in their promise. So Moye rolled up his sleeves and proceeded with the work. First he wired the Stearman people for the location of the center of gravity minus landing wheels. With this information he balanced the pontoons on sawhorses and determined their c.g. By hanging a plumb bob, he got the two c.g.'s in line. The only material he could find for struts was steel tubing used in steam boilers. They worked satisfactorily.

Three months were spent in Singapore. While Moye installed pontoons, Richard brought his writing up to date. Due to impatience and having second thoughts about finding colorful copy in Borneo and the Philippines, Richard suddenly announced he was terminating the world flight.

After weeks of sweating out the installation of the pontoons, Moye felt let down by the sudden decision.

"Look at it this way," he said in a conversation that ran in this vein, "I know there's no archeological ruins in Borneo and the Philippines, and the countries are without classical lore, still—

66 • THEIR EYES ON THE SKIES

The *Flying Carpet* over the Taj Mahal. Since the 1930s, the concepts of Make Believe and Never-Never Lands have given way to lifestyles as foreign as the lands Halliburton and Stephens visited.

we're now equipped to fly on, so let's do so in anticipation something worthwhile will turn up."

In the end Richard was persuaded, and thanks to Moye he found copy to give his book a deserving end.

There is deserved pride in being the first white man to penetrate an unexplored area. While Richard and Moye could not make that claim in Borneo, they nevertheless were the third and fourth white men to venture to head waters of the Rejang River. Together with an English official they penetrated the land of the Dyak headhunters. That is, the Resident official and native servants came by boat, whereas THE FLYING CARPET crew joined them at the village of the chief. Not unlike Northern India, the natives here accepted the airplane as a big bird, and one question was asked: "Does it lay eggs?"

These little people, hardly more than four-and-a-half-feet tall, lived in houses with human heads of slaughtered enemies hanging from the rafters. During the night, when the white men stood up, they learned after the first encounters to avoid bumping against the grisly spoils of war. During the ten-day stay, Moye took the Dyak chief flying. He, in turn, was so grateful he gave the visitors each an armful of heads. To have refused would have been an unpardonable gesture, and yet on the other hand, their bulkiness and weight of some 150 pounds created a shipping problem. To meet the situation, much of their luggage was offered as gifts in return, including a portable phonograph and records. Needless to say, once airborne and away from the Dyaks, the offensive heads went overboard one by one.

Manila. Hong Kong. Yokohama. San Francisco.

Flying into Manila harbor came the distinction of being the second airplane to reach the Philippines from the outside—an Italian flyer had preceded them from Europe. Here THE FLYING CARPET was crated and hoisted aboard the PRESIDENT MCKINLEY. After eighteen months they were homeward bound.

If Richard, during a brief stop at Hong Kong, could have looked into the future, he would have seen himself returning to that city in 1938 with the most grandiose plan yet for adventure. He would build a seagoing Chinese junk and name it "The Sea Dragon." He would sail it to America. It was the beginning of a book he never wrote, for while some 1500 miles at sea he and crew were lost in a typhoon. Richard's affinity for having luck in the face of disaster had run its course.

At San Francisco THE FLYING CARPET was assembled with wheels and flown to Los Angeles. As a tribute to the faithful plane, Richard was to write:

"And now our travels in the air were ended. Moye and I wheeled the old CARPET into a hangar, where bright, impertinently new planes elbowed it for space; and there, for the first time, we realized how much it showed the marks of battle with the elements in a hundred lands. The scarlet was flaked away; the gold tarnished. Scarred, weather-beaten, very worldly-wise, THE FLYING CARPET had returned, a veteran of many conflicts and adventures. But each patch it bore seemed to us like a medal honorably won by the old campaigner, for proved valor and fidelity.

"Honorably won! Through desert and jungle, Africa and Arabia, Himalaya and the islands of the sea ... these brave and sturdy wings, these willing and fleet wings, had brought us safely home."*

In 34 countries Moye had logged 374 hours of flying time to cover 33,660 miles. He had made 168 landings as a landplane in sites of every description, and as a seaplane in a diversity of waters from rivers to open sea.

What became of THE FLYING CARPET?

The same used dealer who had assisted Richard in the beginning sold the plane to two naval officers in Honolulu. Due to faulty installation of its controls during reassembly it crashed on takeoff, killing both officers. The damaged plane was returned to the dealer. Rather than rebuild it, he decided to sell the parts. One wing went for replacement for a plane flying gold out of Honduras. It took five days by ox-cart to get the wing to the stalled plane in the interior. The tail assembly was shipped to Fairbanks, Alaska, for a plane

---

*The Flying Carpet. Bobbs-Merrill Company, 1932.

doing bush work. The polar explorer, Donald B. MacMillan, installed the wheels on his Lockheed Vega. The J5 engine was sold to a flyer in Arizona for his Stinson. The landing struts went to a private plane in Washington state. Other planes acquired the controls and instruments.

As an afterthought it seems a little sad THE FLYING CARPET did not remain intact and end up in a museum. But more saddening are the turbulent changes that have taken place in the world since the Golden Era of Romance. Moye Stephens and Richard Halliburton were the last of the carefree vagabonds. The concepts of Make Believe and Never-Never Lands have given way to lifestyles as foreign as the lands they visited.

4

The Making of a Hero

Tens of thousands of Chinese lined the avenue of sorrow as the cortege passed on a spring day in 1932. Four thousand more appeared at Hungjoa Airdrome to offer tribute at graveside.

The cortege which had rolled slowly from Moore Memorial Church in Shanghai was composed of the hearse, 45 flower-laden cars and 300 more vehicles carrying the leaders of China. Included was T. V. Soong, Minister.

The state funeral honored a national hero of China. But, the man was not Chinese.

He was Robert McCawley Short, American.

More exactly, Colonel Robert Short, American pilot who had died in an air battle defending China against Japan.

Robert McCawley Short was given a state funeral, made a national hero, and posthumously awarded a Colonel's commission because of the deep idealism that burned within him. His death on that fateful day of February 22 was a gallant climax to a lifetime urge to fight—to die if necessary, for the underdog.

By way of analogy Robert Short in his brief span of years was the idealistic All-American Boy. He grew up in Tacoma, Washington, in an era when the lifestyle theme dictated clean living, hard playing, and championing the underdog. Furthermore, there was a great emphasis on succeeding in life. It was a national syndrome shaped by home, church and school. The stories Robert read as a boy echoed and re-echoed character building. Heroes were triumphal in the make-believe worlds because they lived by the rules. Robert Short's whole life was an emulation of his boyhood heroes. He became in turn a hero in his own right.

The Horatio Alger books were inescapable reading for young Americans around the turn of the century. A boy growing up without reading the popular Alger would have been about as rare as one who never played baseball, went swimming, or spent his nickels for picture shows. The plots of the 100 or so Alger books were based on a rags-to-riches formula. Virtue and industry were the inspirational themes. And without exception all heroes were early breadwinners.

Robert, too, was an early breadwinner. In a "strive and succeed" manner he helped support his widowed mother and younger brother by working as a boy messenger in a Tacoma shipyard. In an Alger-like gesture he once gave his mother on Christmas morning the gift of a paid-up delinquent doctor bill.

As Robert advanced through the grammar grades and into high school, he was also somewhat of a prototype of the ever-popular Rover Boys. The adventures of Tom, Dick and Sam through "thick and thin" were to account for a dozen or so books. Actually the series, written by Edward Stratemeyer, was a close second in popularity to the Alger stories. The Rover Boys were given to fun-loving pranks to the delight of millions of readers. Yet, on the serious side, Tom, Dick and Sam were model heroes. They saw to it the mean bully got what he deserved. Moreover, the Rovers came to the rescue—generally in the nick of time, of those in distress. Good prevailed over evil. What better influence was there for boys growing up?

H.F. Hunt, principal of Tacoma's Stadium High, recalls Robert having all the admirable qualities of the storybook hero, although the prankish Rover Boy influence at times proved to be most trying for his teachers.

"Always cheerful and kindly by nature, he would fight for his friends or for anyone he thought was imposed upon. He had many qualities of leadership. He had courage. He was popular with students and teachers alike, although at times he was a frequent source of conference so far as his teachers were concerned."

Actually Robert's main difficulty stemmed from a rather high I.Q. In that respect his behavior, as recognized today, was the lack of a sufficient challenge in school studies to provide a consuming interest. As a foil to boredom, prankishness offered a release. It was in his sophomore year that the continued disruptions reached a crisis. On the recommendation of the teachers, Principal Hunt had little course but to suspend him.

Robert was working as an electrician's helper

when notified he might return to his classes if a letter of recommendation was presented.

With characteristic aplomb, Robert journeyed to the state Capitol. There he sought an audience with the Honorable Louis Hart, Governor of Washington. By his winning smile and infectious personality, he obtained a letter of recommendation from the governor, complete with State Seal.

Back in school he was not a model student, although his behavior was subdued. He excelled in athletics. There were romances that blossomed and faded. At graduation he left a permanent record of prankishness. He appeared on the extreme left and right ends of a panoramic group photo of the senior class.

With high school behind him, he began work with a survey crew on the Cushman Dam under construction. As much as he liked the rugged life in the open, he was faced with a decision with the approach of fall. Should he continue working and ease the financial burden at home? Or should he try making his way through college? College had a strong pull, but the thoughts of the family's sacrifices decided the issue.

With college at least tentatively out of reach he sought self-improvement in correspondence courses. A year or so later, a friend suggested he try for the Army Air Corps Flying Cadet program. Robert investigated the possibilities. What he learned was that candidates for appointment must be unmarried, between 20 and 26 years of age. Those who had not satisfactorily completed at least two years of standard college work must pass a written educational examination. Furthermore, the physical standards were high.

All qualified candidates would be assigned to the Primary Flying School, March Field, Riverside, California. After completion of a six-month course, they would spend an additional half year in advanced training at Kelly Field, San Antonio, Texas. Flying cadets would receive $75 per month, plus a ration allowance of $1 per day. Theirs would be a distinctive uniform.

In addition to hours in the air, flying cadets would receive instruction in theory of flight, airplane engines, aircraft rigging, machine guns, map-making, military law, meteorology, navigation, radio code—in all, 28 subjects necessary for the trained military pilot.

On completion of the course, the flying cadet would be commissioned a Second Lieutenant in the Air Corps Reserve.

The suggestion of the Air Corps program came at a most propitious time. Robert at the moment was caught up in the Lindbergh phenomenon then sweeping the country. Lindbergh's New York to Paris flight and subsequent grand tour of the United States in the SPIRIT OF ST. LOUIS certainly had much to do with his decision.

Along with 28 other candidates he took the written and physical examination at Vancouver Barracks. The hours of self-improvement paid off.

THE MAKING OF A HERO • 77

Robert McCawley Short was given a State funeral, made a national hero of China and posthumously awarded a Colonel's commission because on that fateful day of February 22, 1932, something burned deep inside him—an idealism, an urge to fight—to die, if necessary, for the underdog.

He was one of three selected. At March Field Robert was sworn in with the class of March 1, 1928.

Following dismissal after the swearing in, 245 cadets received their first initiation of Army life. They were ordered to run around the field track. It was a hot day. The inexperience of standing at attention had gotten the best of one youth. Robert noticed the pallor on the boy's face. He whispered he would run in his place. This he did following his own run. The incident was observed by the officer-in-charge. Robert was told, "Short, if you're so anxious to run, keep right on running." He did for another turn around the track.

The cadets, a carefree lot, had come in anticipation of a wonderful year of flying. But that afternoon their ardor was shaken. From the sergeants and enlisted men who served them, they began hearing distressing facts of attrition. Examining boards called "Benzine Boards," convening frequently, would account for two-thirds of the class being "washed out" in primary stage. And of those who were fortunate enough to get to Kelly, the chances were that about one out of ten of the original class would be on hand to receive their wings.

"We live in suspense," Robert wrote in his first letter home.

Primary instruction began the following week in the Consolidated PT-1 biplane trainer. Rather deceiving in appearance, it had under its drum-tight fabric a tubular framework of rugged construction. In the postwar years, thousands of young men got their introduction to flying in a PT-1. And hundreds of patient instructors never got quite used to the bone-shattering landings the ships at times took. The power plant was a modified wartime 180-hp Wright-Hisso. During that first week Robert received 45 minutes of dual instruction.

It was sometime during his third week at March Field that he received his first words of assurance. An instructor making a check flight told him, "Short, you seem to grasp what it's all about."

The ever fear of the "Benzine Board" increased with the tempo of training. One by one, cadets with long faces turned in their gear, made their goodbyes. By nightfall their cots had gone to storage. On March 27, Robert was writing his mother that as yet he had not been called before the board, so for the time being he presumed everything was all right. Mingled with this concern was the deep-seated Alger-boy responsibility. "I will be paid Saturday," he wrote, "and at that time I will send you a check."

A month later he had acquired nearly 20 hours of solo and dual time. He was practicing 80-degree banks, right and left spins, wingovers, chandelles, besides landings and takeoffs. Statistically, the odds of lasting the course were against him, yet the tone of his letters was, "I am resolved to finish." He studied hard, including weekends that were free.

By June the ground school work had increased with the summer temperature. The dreaded board was taking its toll. More than half the class had been sent home. There was no disgrace in the flying cadet being "washed out." On the other hand, there was undeniable honor in lasting out the course; honor of which any cadet might be proud. Those who had survived thus far felt like veterans, although by no means secure.

He had learned a lot in the crowded months at March Field. Not only about airplanes, but more importantly about himself. He found himself growing up. "I sometimes wonder if my rewards haven't been greater in myself than in the material accomplishment of flying," he confided to his mother.

With the approach of graduation, Robert found himself faced with a tough decision. There had developed in the recent months an immediate need to lift the financial burden at home. Now that he was in the top five of the class, Robert believed it was a standing that would assure him a flying job. So his agonizing decision was whether to continue at Kelly Field or ask for a discharge. After much soul-searching he sacrificed his Army career. "It seemed the thing to do," he would say.

Robert's flying ability and likable personality opened doors of opportunity. For several years he was a familiar figure at Southern California airports. He instructed the "Army way," did private flying for the wealthy, had a stint of test piloting for Lockheed, and had the good fortune to be associated with W.B. Kinner, of Kinner Airplane Motors. Eventually, his hometown beckoned. Robert returned to Tacoma to manage the Pierce County Airport. As may have been predicted, his temperament was not a proper foil for political interference. The job lasted nine months. In the meantime he belatedly received his Second Lieutenant's commission in the Air Corps Reserve.

In the great scheme of things, it was the loss of the airport job that set in motion a chain of circumstances that led to a hero's death. For at this opportune time, in answer to previous correspondence, he received a telegram offering him an airmail run in China between Shanghai and Hangchow. The pay was attractive and Robert accepted.

On February 7, 1931, he left Seattle aboard the S.S. PRESIDENT CLEVELAND for Shanghai.

In Shanghai Robert met sickening disappointment. The Loening amphibians he was to fly were nothing more than fugitives from the junk pile. He refused to fly them. Other flying jobs came his way until eventually he was hired by the L.E. Gale Company, a firm marketing American planes in the Orient. As a field representative, his work took him to every province of China as well as to Japan and the Philippines. He became a close friend of T.V. Soong, the minister of China. Soong appointed him an Advisor to the Chinese Air Force.

In the year that passed, his letters home revealed more and more a nature that was not to be deterred. The empathy for his fellowmen and a code of fair dealing that had characterized him since boyhood now played a significant role. Few Americans, he wrote, hardly more than one in fifty, cared to understand the Chinese. The American advisors who had preceded him had shamefully lied and misinformed the Chinese to their own advantage. He was still the All-American Boy who neither smoked nor drank—a living example of the storybook hero.

Robert also felt a deep sense of injustice over the Mukden incident in Manchuria. What happened was a small-scale Pearl Harbor attack in reverse. The Japanese Army leaders stationed at Kwantung belonged to a federation of officers that secretly plotted for an extension of Japanese power. Japanese merchants over the years had invested in the development of Manchuria. The Army clique eyeing the rich agriculture, timber and mineral resources, concluded Japanese expansion should not only begin here, but begin immediately. They staged a fake Chinese bombing raid that knocked out railroad bridges near Mukden. The railroad was a Japanese investment. After vehemently denouncing innocent China to the world, they used the incident as a pretext to take over Manchuria.

With prophetic insight, Robert wrote, "Mother, you cannot realize the brutality and the uselessness of it all and what the United States will have to contend with sometime in the years to come. Japan has no bases of supplies and if the world powers allow her to take Manchuria it won't take ten years to prepare for a world conquest with the United States as the prize."

As the shooting war heated up and the Japanese Army made substantial gains in Manchuria, the Japanese Imperial Navy, jealous of the Army's success, attacked Shanghai.

As the war closed around the International Settlement a mounting fear persisted that trigger-happy Japanese might overrun the area. For days there were tense moments.

"Just now it is nine P.M.," Robert wrote in a letter home, "and the big Hong Kong Bank building clock is striking, and sitting in my office I can hear the bup-bup-bup of machine-gun fire. It isn't steady—just occasional."

From this vantage point he saw the indiscriminate bombing of Shanghai; saw, too, women and children killed. He felt an utter helplessness of not being able to do anything about it. The awful sights and frustrations were a contributing nexus to a fast approaching climax.

The climactic springboard was the arrival of a Boeing fighter. Through Robert's sales work he had succeeded in selling an experimental fighter plane to the Chinese government. At the Boeing plant in Seattle this particular plane had outlived its usefulness. Nevertheless X-66W, c/n 1260 was the proven prototype for the United States Army P-12E and Navy F4B-3 series. In appearance it was a single-seat biplane with metal monocoque fuselage, and powered with a 450-hp Pratt & Whitney engine. Its speed was in excess of 200 miles per hour. The outstanding P-12s developed from this particular testbed marked an era in pursuit development.

In contrast to such a superior fighter, the Air Force of the Chinese Central Government was a conglomeration of obsolete American and European planes. Russian advisors had organized the Air Force in 1927, thus the mainstay of planes were the Soviet-built De Havilland 9A's of 1918 design. By American standards not only were the Chinese planes inferior, but also the pilots were totally lacking in flying proficiency. The only Chinese pilot capable of flying the Boeing was Col. T.S. Shen, who had trained at Kelly.

At the badly bombed Hungjoa airdrome outside Shanghai, the P-12 was uncrated and assembled. In the dawn of an early morning Robert made the test flight. After taxiing to the runway, he made a check of instruments and controls. When satisfied, he advanced the throttle. Almost as soon as the fighter got rolling, it came off the ground in a jackrabbit hop. The P-12, he discovered, was a "hot" airplane.

Following the test flight, the Chinese insignia of a 12-point white star on a light blue circle was painted on the fuselage of olive-drab color. Because the three-hour flight to Nanking could be interrupted by roving Japanese patrols, machine-gun belts were threaded into the twin Brownings.

When all was ready, Robert took off.

The date was February 19, 1932. He had 36 hours to live.

The route to Nanking took him over villages where Japanese Navy bombers had made ruthless war. Somewhere along the route—possibly shortly after leaving Shanghai, he was spotted by Lieutenant Tokoro leading a reconnaissance flight. The three planes in Tokoro's command were Mitsubishi, BIM, type 13, 2-place, single-engine biplane bombers. Besides the pilot, each machine carried a rear gunner. The BIMs, as well as all Navy planes operating in that area, were attached to the carrier KAGA.

Tokoro was flying at about 10,000 feet when he saw and recognized a P-12 flying in a westerly direction. The P-12 was flying at the same altitude, and on a course that would bring it within shooting distance of the Japanese. Through the Japanese spy system, the P-12 was known to Navy Intelligence. What was not known was the plane's performance. At the moment Tokoro assumed the American fighter was being flown by a Chinese. The Japanese contempt for Chinese pilot skill, and the fact they were three against one, offered an excellent combat opportunity. Accordingly, they closed in for the kill.

Robert met the challenge by pushing the throttle forward, easing back on the stick and standing the P-12 on its tail. Over his shoulder he saw the Japanese making a feeble attempt to climb to meet him. After gaining 1500 feet altitude he executed a fast wingover and came diving down on his adversaries.

Now it must be recognized that Robert had had no combat training. Had he gone to Kelly Field for advanced training he would have had machine-gun firing at moving targets, together with simulated air battles. As he came diving out of the sky, lining his sights on a forward adversary, he would in the moments ahead be his own self-appointed instructor.

The P-12's excessive speed carried Robert past the lead bomber, and whether or not his short burst found its target he knew not. He pulled up and away from the Japanese who were turning to meet him. In the next few minutes, as Robert's combat maneuvers and shooting improved, Tokoro realized that the other was fast gaining the upper hand and shortly they were going to be shot down, one by one, unless—Tokoro resorted to the old World War I trick of each plane fastening itself on the tail of another, making and flying a continuous circle. The Lufbery circle it was called. With the rear gunners firing at Robert as he dived in, they were reasonably protected. For five minutes the air battle continued with neither Robert nor the Japanese gaining an advantage despite the amount of ammunition spent. Finally, after making a last futile dart, Robert broke off the engagement and set his course for Nanking. When he arrived only one bullet hole was located in the plane.

Due to faulty communications Robert's trip to Nanking was unnecessary. For what was not known at Shanghai was that the squadrons stationed at Nanking had moved to Soochow. From a military standpoint the planes could now operate within 50 miles of Shanghai against the Japanese land forces overrunning the country. Against the Japanese Air Force they were hopelessly outclassed, and thus avoided battle.

Either that day or the next, Robert backtracked to Soochow. Here at the Hangam airdrome he found antiquated planes carefully concealed under camouflage nettings. Quickly the Boeing was wheeled out of sight.

Soochow was a paralyzed city. The Japanese spy system, with swift efficiency, reported train movements and river shipping. Japanese carrier planes operating off a land airstrip took only a few minutes to fly the short distance.

For several days the train bound for Shanghai had been delayed. It was not a military train. Rather, it was made up mainly of civilians attempting to escape the expected coming of Japanese forces. With each day's delay more civilians arrived with scanty possessions. Against better judgment the train officials decided at length to make a run for it. The date of departure was February 22.

In America on this date a holiday spirit prevailed. In keeping with tradition a lot of cherry pie was being eaten in memory of George Washington's birthday. But in faraway China the thoughts at Soochow were whether or not the bombers would come.

That the train was overflowing with non-combatants was of heartless indifference to the spies. The bombing of it would be ruthless slaughter. A few more casualties in the toll of thousands. Fifteen minutes after the train's departure, or, to be precise, at 4:20 P.M., three Japanese bombers appeared on the horizon. They were flying at 2700 feet altitude slightly above a scattering of cloud covering.

While details are somewhat confusing, nevertheless the scene at Hangam can be reasonably pictured. The consequences of the oncoming bombers burned deeply into Robert's inner conscience. His life pattern of acting impetuously for noble causes triggered the decision to give battle to the Japanese. He ordered the Boeing out of its hiding.

"*Quai-ti! Quai-ti!* (Faster! Faster!)" he urged the mechanics.

He was in the cockpit donning helmet and goggles when the crank was inserted in the inertia starter. Over his shoulder he could see the bombers closing in.

"Contact!"

He released the inertia starter. The propeller revolved, hesitated—then caught to become a whirling disc. Without waiting for a warmup, Robert released the brake. At full power and a brief run the Boeing was off the grassy field. A climbing turn brought him in line of the bombers.

Not until Robert had gained nearly 1000 feet of altitude, not until then was the P-12 spotted by the Japanese. Lieutenant Sakinaga, leading the trio, immediately began swinging in a curve to the left. The change in direction permitted three Japanese fighter planes that were following some distance in the rear at an altitude of 4500 feet to close the gap between them. The fighter planes were Japan's finest. The Sunshiki Nigo Kansai was copied from the British Gloster Gambit. It was a single-seat biplane with a top speed of 144 miles per hour. The armament was two 7.7mm machine guns. The planes were also attached to the carrier KAGA.

Robert was totally unaware of the Japanese fighter planes. All reasoning points to this. While climbing to meet the bombers, had he taken a precautionary survey of the sky, it is possible the scattering of clouds could have at any moment blocked the line of sight. Certainly his ignoring the fighters should confirm the belief he was not aware of the greater odds against him. Further-

(Above) The ill-fated Boeing P-12 Robert Short flew to immortality. This photograph was made at the Boeing Company prior to its shipment to China.

(Below) The distinction of shooting down Japan's first adversary in an aerial battle is credited to 27-year-old Lieutenant Nokiji Ikuta pictured on the left.

THE MAKING OF A HERO • 91

more, he was entering the battle handicapped by not having a protective wingman. And all the while he was climbing the bombers were swinging inwardly to the advantage of the fighter planes.

As Robert came within shooting distance he locked his sights on one adversary. He pressed the electric button on the stick. The two fixed, synchronized .30 caliber Brownings erupted a torrent of steel-jacketed bullets. Bullets pierced the left leg of Lieutenant Hajime Sasaki, who did double duty of radio operator and rear gunner. The momentum of the full-bore climb carried the P-12 through and above the bombers.

With the advantage of height, Robert peeled off in a diving turn. Down he came sweeping across the line of flight of a bomber flown by Lieutenant Sakinaga. The bullets raked the machine, killing rear gunner Lieutenant Sosumu Kotani, destined to be the first Japanese to die in aerial combat.

Unknown to Robert (otherwise he would have taken evasive action) the fighter planes had closed the gap and were diving on him.

Leading the trio was 27-year-old Nokiji Ikuta. He began firing at 150 meters. The first shots hit the tail assembly. Parts of it flew back into the slipstream. Ikuta moved the stick slightly and the stream of bullets began stitching the length of the Boeing.

Still closing, Ikuta was only 50 meters away when he saw the pilot throw up his hands—a pilot Ikuta believed to be Chinese. He saw two white smoke trails from the stricken plane as it began to fall off. The white smoke erupted into red fire as the machine began revolving to the left. Ikuta followed the descent long enough to see the Boeing crash in the vicinity of the Woosung Forts.

The dogfight as such marked Japan's first aerial battle in which an enemy plane was shot down.

Robert McCawley Short came to China as just another American. In the year he lived there, he endeared himself to the people, largely because he was not there to exploit them or to humble them with superior white-man ways. With genuine sincerity he contributed his know-how to make China a better place. In gratitude for his unselfishness, and in particular for the chivalrous deed, the Chinese government honored his memory with a posthumous Colonel's commission and a State funeral that was delayed until his mother and brother Edmond could attend.

An impressive monument was erected over his grave. The Chinese went to the New Testament to find adequate words to express their feelings for the valiant American who gave his life for an alien cause. The inscription on the shaft, in Chinese characters, reads: "Greater love hath no man than this, that he lay down his life for his friends."

5

Wings of Mercy

In the rugged, wooded wilderness around Medford, Oregon, only two forms of transportation have ever worked really well: mules and airplanes.

Most of the mules are gone. The airplane remains to serve as a combination Santa Claus and Florence Nightingale for thousands of Southern Oregonians and Northern Californians who choose to live and work so far from civilization that a cry for help can easily go unheard.

Unheard, that is, except for a businesslike group of flying Samaritans called, prosaically, "Mercy Flights, Inc."

They fly out of the Medford Municipal Airport. One man, George Milligan, usually is at the controls or in the tower watching the takeoffs of the four planes bearing the red cross of medical mercy. The story of Mercy Flights must necessarily be built around the motivating spirit of George Milligan.

In 1949 Milligan came to Medford as a CAA towerman. When he heard the frantic calls asking for doctors and ambulances over the shortwave radio, he felt utter helplessness. He was a pilot, thinking as an airman would. In each instance, on hearing distress calls, he spotted the origin of the plea on the tower map. Then he translated the distance to the nearest hospital in terms of air time.

"Look at this," he would point out to the other towermen as they crowded about the sectional map with its mass of contour lines and color shadings. "Look at this," he would repeat, and

The infectious George Milligan smile that parlayed a dream into a reality.

with his finger pinpoint where it appeared a plane could land. It might be a narrow valley or a sandbar on one of the rivers. Still studying the map, he would talk on. "What this community needs is a volunteer rescue operation. I'd be willing to volunteer as a pilot."

"Yeah, George, sounds like a great idea."

"Yeah, George, somebody should do something about it."

"Yeah, George. . . ."

Weeks passed, and the frantic calls continued, and each time Milligan spotted the remote area and speculated. The ignoring of the obvious solution bothered him no end. However, he continued to talk about it to his friends. But, as is often the case in matters of civic neglect, nothing was done.

That is, nothing was done until Art Winetrout, an auto dealer, died.

Stricken with polio, Winetrout was rushed by car ambulance to Portland. En route, several stops were made to give him oxygen. The journey took 12 hours. The lengthy travel time and the delays were beyond the endurance of the weakened victim.

Milligan was shocked. He was shocked by the waste of life in an airplane age. "I could have flown him to Portland in 90 minutes," he said.

As a newcomer to Medford, young Milligan knew relatively few persons. None of those he knew were prominent in the community. He had never met the newspaper editor. Nor had he met the mayor, or the civic leaders. Nevertheless, with hat in hand, he approached these persons in order.

"Offhand, the idea is great," editor Eric Allen, Jr., of the *Mail Tribune* told him, "but I happen to know air ambulances have been tried in other communities and it just didn't work out financially. Still—," he pondered for a moment, "why don't you talk this over with Mayor Diamond Flynn. Maybe, just maybe, we might make a go of it here."

"Great idea, George," the mayor told him. "I'm going to have you talk with—" He wrote the names of several civic leaders on a scratch pad. "Talk with them and get their feelings on a volunteer rescue service."

George Milligan may be characterized as being deceptive in appearance and mannerism. He has a casualness that covers a tremendous under-the-surface drive. Call it visionary. Call it an ordinary guy trying to get a job done, but young Milligan, uneasy in his new role, began talking with everyone who would listen. He talked to civic groups. He talked to women's organizations and to school groups. Importantly, he talked to the man on the street. He told them what they already knew. People were suffering, and some dying, for lack of an aerial ambulance service. Everyone he talked to had friends or relatives who had suffered, greatly. Not surprisingly, he found many who were skeptical of the idea. They pointed out, as editor Allen did, air ambulances had been tried elsewhere and found too costly to survive. Milligan shrugged off the adverse talk. Because, by now, his missionary zeal was burning like an afterburner on takeoff. He kept right on talking.

Thanks to the young man's zeal, $3000 was raised, including $1000 by school children. A nonprofit organization called Mercy Flights became a reality. George Milligan was chosen chairman. A war-surplus Cessna could be had for $2400. After it was purchased, $300 was spent for a radio compass. The balance of the money went for ambulance equipment. Five pilots, including Milligan, volunteered their services.

The inception of Mercy Flights could not have been more timely. The great polio epidemic was sweeping the country. When the killer disease was hitting the hardest, 78 polio victims were flown to Portland. Although no flights were turned down, there were times Milligan didn't know where the next gallon of gas was coming from. Within a year, Mercy Flights, as some had predicted, was in a financial tailspin.

With dim hopes of recovery, young Milligan was understandably half sick with frustration. It wasn't fair to have Mercy Flights fold after it had proved its worth—had saved lives. Well meaning friends tried to console him, telling him he had done his best. It wasn't his fault the project failed.

Milligan refused to accept defeat. In his mind he knew there was bound to be a solution. In the days ahead a hundred ideas germinated. Speedily they were rejected as impractical—that is, all but one.

Why not, Milligan reasoned, promote a family insurance plan? For a low-cost premium a member of the family would be entitled to 400 miles of one-way emergency flight. A distance of 400 miles put the hospitals of San Francisco and Seattle within reach. The hitch was it was going to take a lot of family participation to pay the cost of a few. Would the public go for such a plan? With the tanks of the Cessna dry and the need of an engine overhaul, Milligan was willing to grasp the proverbial straw. After checking out the legal aspects, the Board of Directors gave their okay.

The Milligan plan offered ambulance service to families within a 150-mile radius of Medford. The towns within the area got to know the persuasive young man who came and shook hands with everyone and told them Mercy Flights was "here to stay."

At first the insurance money just dribbled in. But each time a polio or accident victim was lifted from an isolated community and within relatively few minutes was in a modern hospital, the need became more convincing, especially to holdouts. When the financial situation eased, Milligan turned his attentions to another need.

The twin-engine Cessna was fine for long hauls, but it was not suitable for short meadows and sandbars that often faced a mountain wall.

Such landings and takeoffs held terrors for the pilots who risked their lives to save a life. To make the ambulance service more practical, Milligan told the Board of Directors, "What is needed is a plane that will go only where birds dare to fly."

"What do you have in mind, George?" he was asked.

"A Piper Super Cruiser with 150-horsepower engine with PA-14 flaps, modified to take a stretcher patient."

They called it BAND AID—this Super Cruiser that in time performed wonders.

Take the time Milligan went to Agness, an isolated settlement on the Rogue River.

It wasn't an airstrip really. Just a meadow on the side of a mountain for pasturing cows. It wasn't straight. It wasn't level. The turbulence was known to be plenty bad. A couple of planes had cracked up when gusts died and left them stranded 40 feet above the slope.

Milligan got BAND AID down at Agness on a power landing. Fortunately there were no cows to dispute the rollout, although several were in the nearby brush. It was a short walk down the slope to the settlement. After delivering urgent medicine he found, on returning, the cows in some perverse way had decided to make it difficult to take off. He would chase them into the brush but by the time he returned to the plane and warmed it up, the cows were back on the airstrip. This happened a couple of times.

Where the downwind end of the pasture ended there was about 200 feet to the first bend. Beyond was perhaps 500 feet to where the cows insisted on being. In between were ups and downs of the terrain with more of it upward than down. Milligan scratched his head as he studied the layout. After carefully eyeballing the distance he was pretty certain if he got around the bend with built-up speed he would clear the cows on liftoff. Still he hesitated, and then the words of an old-time mail pilot came to mind. "When in doubt, make up your mind and stick to it. Don't drive yourself crazy wondering if you've made the right decision. Chances are ten to one what you decide will be right."

That settled it. He would try. And thus was born a discovery of how to get BAND AID off postage-stamp-sized fields and sandbars.

With the tail of the plane among the trees, Milligan held the brakes tight. He dropped the flaps, ran the engine full up, raised the tail in the slipstream, then snapped off the brakes. The Super Cruiser leaped forward. Despite rudder control it began drifting toward a fence at the bend. At the last moment he saw that the right wing was on the verge of clipping posts. Instinctively he put the stick over to drop the right aileron. Hopefully he would lift the wing sufficiently to clear the posts. And he did. With the aileron acting as an extended flap the wing lifted, but more than that, the right wheel broke from the ground.

Half of BAND AID was airborne.

With half the plane flying, Milligan quickly reversed the stick procedure to give an extended flap to the left wing. It worked. BAND AID became airborne completely. He had taken off in slightly over 200 feet. Later he learned by using this method he could take off in 350 feet with a patient.

Someday perhaps Hollywood will make a movie featuring Mercy Flights. When they do there will be plenty of drama to build on. All that will be lacking for the storyline will be the love interest, and supplying that would be no great chore for professional script writers.

The writers will likely make use of incidents where Mercy Flights missions raced the stork to the hospital; also landing on highways blocked off by the Highway Patrol to pick up auto victims. And of course, the dramatic air rescue would be a must.

The air rescue begins with George Milligan and Victor Seeberger working the day watch in the Medford tower. It was one of those Oregon winter days with a fairly low overcast. There were frequent snow squalls and at best a visibility of two miles. The top of the overcast was reported at 2500 feet.

At 12:51 Seattle ARTC Center phoned. Milligan took the call.

"Hey, you fellows down there. There's a plane calling Medford on center frequency. Sounds urgent. Got it—?"

"Got it. Thanks." Milligan switched to 122.2 frequency. What he heard was, ". . . why doesn't someone answer at Medford—"

"This is Medford. Go ahead."

"We're lost. . . . We don't know where we are." There was a note of panic in the man's voice.

"Take it easy. What is your gas situation?"

"What's that you said?"

"How much gasoline do you have?"

"Oh, gas . . . let's see—"

There followed what seemed an unreasonable delay. Milligan was about to repeat when the voice came on.

"Looks like one tank is empty. . . . The other, it's almost empty." There was stark fright in the man's voice when he asked, "What'll we do?"

During this brief exchange of words, Seeberger, using a radio direction finder, got a "line of position" reading on the plane. While the towermen now had a directional reading, what was not known was how far away the aircraft was on the position line.

"Now listen . . . do you hear?"

"I hear you."

"Wherever you are, we're going to get you to Prospect. The weather is clear at Prospect. What is your heading?"

"Heading? I don't know. I'm not a pilot."

"What!"

"I don't know how to fly. The pilot is a deaf mute. I talk to him with hand signals."

The immensity of the plight struck home to the two towermen. Position unknown. Amount of gas low. Pilot situation in doubt.

"God help them," muttered Seeberger.

At once some ray of hope came from two separate aircraft over western Oregon. Each was tuned in. Immediately both pilots volunteered to begin searching. The talker of the distressed plane said to look for a red and white Cessna. "But hurry," he said. "We don't have much gas."

In an exchange of conversation Milligan learned that neither of the searching aircraft had a direction finder. Without this aid, only by sheer luck would either locate the Cessna. With precious moments being lost, Milligan made a decision. He would join the search in the Mercy Flights Twin Beech. It was equipped with a direction finder.

Turning the mike over to Seeberger, he raced down the steps to the ground level and sprinted the hundred yards to where the Twin Beech was kept on emergency standby. After a hasty warm-up he took off. Above the overcast was sparkling sky. Here was a world of rugged peaks protruding above a sea of clouds. It was a small matter to locate the Cessna. The white Mercy Flight plane with the huge red crosses pulled up alongside. Across the distance Milligan saw immense relief on the faces of two men and a woman. Making a sweeping turn he headed for Prospect. Out of the corner of his eye he saw the Cessna turn to follow.

Milligan knew the appearances of relief were tentative at best, especially with the talker pressing the mike button, opening the circuit and blurting, "How much further? The needle says empty."

"Ten minutes . . . ten minutes, I say. Did the gauge just now reach empty?"

"I think so . . . I don't know. We were looking for you."

"Airplane tanks have a back-up reserve. . . . You understand?" Then, not betraying his own doubts, he added, "Hang in there. You'll make it."

The minutes passed, agonizingly slowly.

Milligan's attempts at voicing encouragement only met with anguished responses. Still he felt that now and then he had to say something, if for no other reason than to offer a foil to their emotional struggles.

Nearing Prospect came thin spots in the overcast. There were glimpses of the Rogue River gorge threading into the Cascade Mountains. Then came more and more open cloud areas, revealing endless pines blanketing the mountainsides. Finally there appeared a slash in the forest a mile away. It was the airstrip haven at Prospect.

With audible relief the Cessna talker blurted, "We see it . . . we see it."

But—

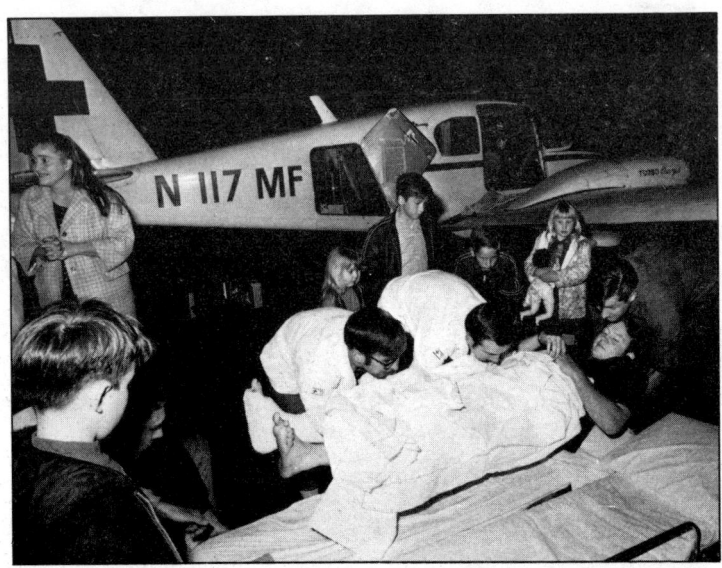

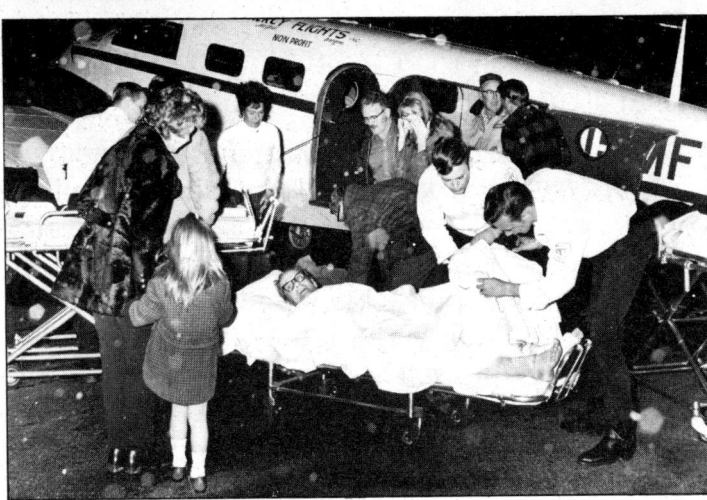

Night or day, Mercy Flights, Inc., is available for those in distress.

The next instant the voice erupted. "The engine's missing... now it's picking up." There was a long pause. "It's missing again... missing and picking up..."

Milligan saw the propeller erratically windmilling and picking up and windmilling again, the final symptoms of gas exhaustion. Gauging the line of the Cessna's descent, he realized the odds against making it safely down were that of the ball taking the final bounce on the roulette wheel.

With the Cessna sinking lower and lower, Milligan involuntarily was holding his breath and bracing himself against the emotional shock of seeing an airplane crash.

It was then, as if by God's will, the engine caught.

Moreover, it kept on running, giving forth life-giving rpm's.

Now the Cessna had a chance. No longer was it sinking, but was leveled out. It held altitude until the engine abruptly cut out again.

Milligan saw the propeller again windmilling. Once more the plane was sinking. But just when it looked as if the plane was going to crash, the engine caught momentarily.

This time the pickup of rpm's was enough to clear the airstrip's outer boundary. The pilot didn't flare out. He flew the Cessna right to the ground. It bounced hard, bounced again, and was safely down on the runway.

By the time Milligan landed, braked, turned

around and taxied back, the three passengers were out of the plane. All too noticeable were their lingering expressions of the deep fear experienced, mingled with God-given relief. It was then that Milligan discovered a fourth passenger. In the back seat, strapped in a back pack, was a year-old baby, smiling and innocent of the ways of fate.

The script writers of the Mercy Flights movie would save the BIG scene until last. That would be the dramatic events of Christmas week, 1952. It was a week of few Christmas carols in western Oregon. Rather, what was heard were prayers for help from communities being isolated by angry floods. The winter so far had been one of the wettest in Oregon history. Rain, sleet, snow, and more rain had fallen during the weeks of early winter. There seemed to be no letup. Every creek ran bank full, and this collective water poured into rivers that in turn washed away some settlements and isolated others. Hardest hit were those on the Rogue River.

The Rogue River families were totally dependent on a weekly mail boat for supplies. Understandably, the mail boat wasn't running. Grub and necessities were running low. On Christmas Eve thoughts of the river people didn't dwell on Santa Claus; instead, they were wondering how much longer they could hold out.

All through the history of mankind, Samaritans have stepped forth to help their fellowmen in times of need. At noon, December 24th, Fred Hale, a flying service operator located at Grants Pass, loaded his light plane with sacks of food. He would make aerial drops to the beleaguered settlements. Darkness that afternoon came earlier than usual because of another storm moving in from the coast. By the time darkness closed in, Hale had not returned. It was certain he was down somewhere. Mercy Flights was called.

George Milligan volunteered to fly a search flight.

It's going to be rough, he reminded himself as he fired up the Beech. He'd be flying down a twisting river on a dark night. Flying into a storm mass, where mountains rose abruptly for 5000 feet. All he could hope to find would be a signal fire.

And he wasn't sure he'd be able to follow the river. When he picked up Grants Pass he found a faint sliver of reflection off the water. That would be all he had for a guide. It took guessing at times, but he managed to hold to the twisting course. Some 25 miles downstream he spotted a fire flaring up dead ahead. Fresh fuel was being added. Was it a signal from Hale? In response Milligan blinked his landing lights off and on. Not certain this signal was from Hale he flew on. When he became engulfed in clouds and snow, he climbed out and flew back to Grants Pass. Again he began a low-level flight downstream. Again he spotted the fire. Again it blazed up. Now he was certain it was a Hale signal. Too dark to see below, he climbed and circled above the mountains. An Air Force radar site vectored on him. "You're over Black Bar Lodge," the voice out of the night told him. This was one of the places Hale was to drop food.

Now the drama unfolded tailor-made for a script writer's plot.

Despite the storn increasing in fury during the night, two rivermen decided to brave the swollen, raging current in a small boat. If they could make it to Black Bar Lodge, they would take Hale on downstream to Gold Beach at river's mouth. They set out at dawn. Following the boat's progress from the air was pilot Ed Scholz of the U.S. Forest Service. The pickup of Hale was made at Black Bar Lodge, but rough water forced an abandonment of the journey downstream at the isolated lodge of Marial. Prearranged signals flashed to Scholz indicated that Hale was injured and needed a doctor.

Scholz returned to Grants Pass where Dr. B.E. Nikkelson volunteered to go to the aid of Hale. The Forest Service plane was inadequate for landing at Marial, so Scholz borrowed Mercy Flight's BAND AID. But the pilot and doctor found on returning to the canyon that Marial was socked in with low overcast. Continuing on, they found a hole above Paradise Bar. A landing was made on a grassy strip. They were seven miles from Marial.

Carrying a portable radio, Scholz and Nikkelson hiked upstream to Marial. In the meantime an arrangement was made to have the Twin Beech arrive and circle to accept radiophone messages. At the appointed hour in a storm buffeting the plane piloted by Milligan he learned, as he circled at 10,000 feet, an account of Hale's accident.

Hale had made one successful drop of food packages at Black Bar Lodge. He was coming in low for a second drop when a downdraft slammed the plane into the trees directly behind the lodge building. The wings were sheared off. The plane exploded in flame. In frantic desperation, Hale clawed his way through the fabric. He tumbled out with clothes afire. He had sustained bad burns on his hands and head. His eyes were swollen shut. There was only aspirin at the lodge to relieve pain.

Despite the agonizing pain, Hale urged the making of a signal fire with plenty of standby fuel. This was done and the lodge people had all but given up when they heard the Twin Beech in the darkness. Hope was greatly renewed when Milligan made a second pass, even though the storm was closing in.

The seriousness of Hale's condition, with no early promise of weather letup, prompted a rescue operation to be attempted on the ground. Bulldozers would cut a trail over the mountains. It would be an almost impossible task, but at least loggers working around the clock would give it a try. Another try would be made from the air at the first favorable break in the weather. This time it would be by helicopter. In answer to a plea, the commanding officer of McChord Air Force Base, Tacoma, Washington, agreed to send a chopper. Mercy Flights would rendezvous twice daily over Marial for an exchange of messages.

Monday the storm raged on with no signs of letting up. The phone rang at the Mercy Flights office. The call was from Grants Pass.

"One of our radio operators talked with a ham in Crescent City [a California city on the coast near the Oregon state line]. Klamath has been wiped out by flood waters. The people got out okay, but right now they're jam-packed in the high school gym at Crescent City. They need blankets and supplies, but mostly blankets. We'll scrounge the blankets. Right now volunteers are gathering them. Here's the situation at Crescent City. There's no communications except by ham radio. There's no way getting into Crescent City except by plane..."

Milligan, back from an early morning rendezvous over Marial, gassed the Twin Beech and flew through a downpour of rain to Grants Pass. Two pickup trucks with blankets were parked in the opening of a hangar. Volunteers in rain gear were standing by. While the blankets were stowed aboard, Milligan gave them the latest on Hale, which was not good. Dr. Nikkelson had reported Hale's condition was deteriorating.

"Did you see the loggers?" someone asked.

Yes, he had. He had seen the snakelike track over seemingly impossible terrain where they had pushed bulldozers—one dragging an ambulance—over rockslides, fallen timbers, and somehow had crossed swollen creeks. They still had a long way to go.

"Those guys must be tearing up a hundred thousand dollars' worth of equipment," another commented. It was an assumption that proved to be true.

Climbing out of Grants Pass, Milligan made the run to Crescent City. Here much of the lowlands was a vast sea. En route back to Medford he picked up a radio call for himself. It was the Mercy Flights' office. A teenage girl was stricken with polio and would have to be flown immediately to the clinic at Eugene, Oregon. The rain had turned to sleet when the girl, bundled in a stretcher, was lifted aboard. Wing icing and headwinds slowed the flight, so much so that on the turnaround, Milligan was late for the afternoon rendezvous.

Meanwhile at the appointed hour, Dr. Nikkelson and others, amid the lashing of wind and downpour of rain, found they were unable to contact Milligan by radio. Not knowing whether they could hear a plane above the wails of storm, they feared the radio batteries had become too weak for signal strength. Nevertheless, they continued to stand by, straining to catch the familiar engine drone. Finally, a half-hour later, they heard the gunning of engines and changing of propeller pitch, a means used to attract their attention. The batteries proved okay and from Milligan they learned that the Air Force helicopter had reached Roseburg, where it was grounded by the storm. The fact that a whirlybird was only an hour's flying time away did much to cheer the beleaguered party.

By Tuesday, the third day, the storm showed signs of breaking up. In the meantime, the bone-tired loggers, working around the clock for two days and not bothering to give proper maintenance to the equipment, had managed to bulldoze a trail of sorts to Black Bar Lodge. The helicopter was still grounded at Roseburg. A word from its pilot created a new development. Through a misunderstanding they were without a radio that would work either Marial or a Mercy Flights plane. What was needed was a portable radio with VHF band. Furthermore, they wanted a map of the Rogue River area. With a map and radio they would leave at the first instance of cloud breakup and fly over the mountain range to Marial.

George Milligan studied the wall map at the Mercy Flights office. Getting to Roseburg with a Forest Service map and a portable radio would take some doing, especially with the Roseburg weather too low for an instrument approach. However, the more he studied the map, the more it seemed there was a way.

Yes, he believed it could be done. He would fly Highway Interstate 5 and stay below the cloud ceiling. The road had a lot of turns, most of them were more or less gentle, and there were a lot of ups and downs. One of the ups might just reach into the ceiling. In that case he would zoom straight up into the overcast and get on top. Doing so would of course scrub the flight. The possibility of sufficient ceiling all the way to Roseburg was worth a try. It would help, too, if he had someone along familiar with the landmarks. He turned to his secretary. "Please get me the State Highway Patrol."

The westwardly flight to Grants Pass with a volunteer patrolman riding in the copilot's seat was under plenty of ceiling. Here they turned north. Thereafter it was noticeable that each "up" was taking them closer to the ceiling. On approaching the Wolf Creek area, Milligan succeeded in raising Marial. He learned what he suspected—the helicopter would never find Marial coming over the mountains. He was advised to have the helicopter work its way to the coast and begin at the mouth of the Rogue River, working its way upstream to Marial.

The patrolman, having driven this beat for many years, was a great help. Recognizing landmarks that would suddenly emerge in the gloom, he cautioned what to expect next. When the ceiling closed down to less than 200 feet the situation was acute. The mountains on either side were

116 • THEIR EYES ON THE SKIES

(Above) The modified Piper Super Cruiser, affectionately called *Band Aid,* could take off where only birds dare fly.

(Below) The end of an ordeal. George Milligan (left) assists in final airlift operation of badly burned George Hale.

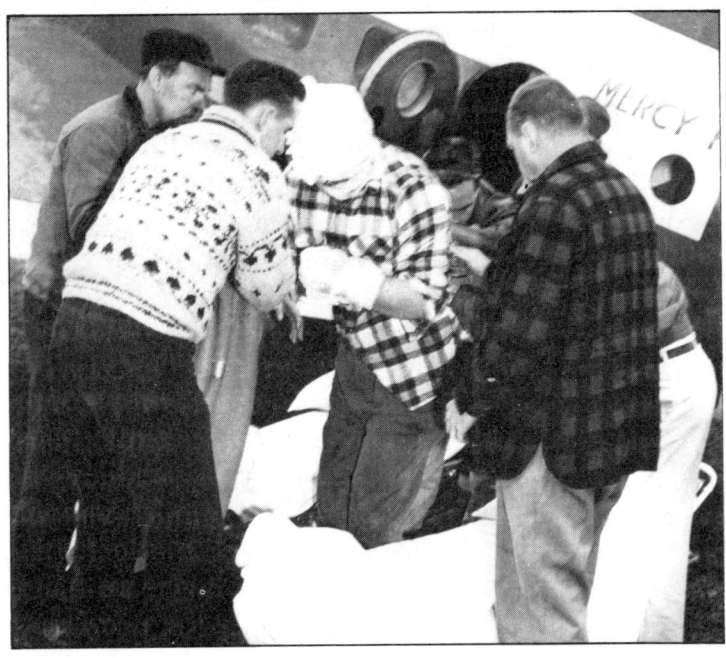

2000 feet higher. Milligan pulled the throttles wide open. He explained, "I'll need all the power I can get to clear these mountains if we find ourselves running into the overcast."

And so for the last 20 miles he flew at full throttle. With the help of the patrolman they reached the Roseburg airport. It was another crisis surmounted in the days of one crisis following another.

Although the storm was breaking up, there was yet no sun. Wednesday was another gloomy day with fog blanketing western Oregon. Feeling its way, the helicopter made it to the coast, then swung south. By late afternoon when Milligan made his final rendezvous he reported the 'copter had reached Gold Beach at the mouth of the Rogue River. For the long-suffering Fred Hale, this was the most enlightening news in four days. It meant he could practically count on rescue Thursday morning.

Thursday morning events moved swiftly. The loggers, dirty, wet, unshaven, with faces haggard and eyes red without sleep, broke through the last barrier. The ambulance, battered and scarred, came to rest before the lodge at Marial. It was a symbol of victory of sorts, for in the distance was heard the approaching helicopter.

The 'copter carried the patient to North Bend. There it was met by Milligan in the Twin Beech. He in turn flew Hale to the hospital at Grants Pass, arriving there during a drenching rain.

A quarter century has passed since young Milligan took his hat in hand and approached the Medford city fathers. Some 5000 mercy flights have been flown. In terms of lives saved, in suffering eased, in anxiety calmed, who can tally the results? Mercy Flights, in the meantime, weathered many a storm, literally and financially. There was one storm that brought Mercy Flights to the brink of termination. It deserves telling, yet reveals a shameful episode of government bureaucracy.

In 1971 the Federal Aviation Administration, known as the FAA, in an unrealistic approach, declared Mercy Flights must be grounded because it did not conform to Air Taxi Service regulations. A hearing was held at Medford.

Mercy Flights spokesmen, including George Milligan, pointed out that Air Taxi regulations were written with no thought for the kind of lifesaving operations by Mercy Flights. No landings could be made at nights on unlighted airstrips. No landings could be made on highways to pick up accident victims. No missions flown under extreme weather conditions. To be specific, of all the mercy flights flown in its 22 years of activity, perhaps half were flown under instrument conditions prohibited by Air Taxi regulations. There were other logical objections—the most ruinous would be the certainty of Mercy Flights losing its nonprofit status and tax exemptions.

During the two days the hearing officer and his

panel of colleagues heard an outpouring of support coming from the whole length of the southern Oregon coast. In all, thousands of names were represented in personal testimony, affidavits, letters and petitions, including endorsement of Mercy Flights by Governor Tom McCall and Senator Mark Hatfield. Now, one would think that with the logical evidence presented, plus the real issue of human lives being saved, that the FAA would have lent a sympathetic ear. But such was not the case.

Before the hearing ended the FAA representatives, with their stubborn backs up, gave every indication that they were out to ground Mercy Flights. All logical objections were swept aside. Finally, as feared, a tentative finding was issued. Mercy Flights must be grounded.

The reaction was immediate and forthcoming in the right places. The governor, both senators, and the four congressmen got into the act. Everyone in the FAA hierarchy from the Administrator on down soon realized that they had "an Oregon bear by the tail."

With the public spotlight on FAA, the tables were turned. FAA was now on trial.

Why, the public demanded, had FAA waited 22 years to bring charges? If Mercy Flights was in the wrong, then wasn't FAA negligent during those 22 years? One official confided the FAA never before had met such a concentration of public interest. These denunciations grew in clamor until at last Robert Whittington, assistant FAA administrator, flew to Medford to take a good look at Mercy Flights' operations. His visit proved to be the turning point.

In the end FAA agreed to write new regulations for non-profit ambulance services. Their final decision makes one wonder in sober reflection why the FAA took the route they did. After all, their representatives could have met with Mercy Flights representatives in some back room and, over a few cups of coffee, reached a similar agreement.

There are no medals or national honors for George Milligan and his kind. No Hall of Fame in which his name might be enshrined. This omission is certainly a pity. Someday hopefully deserved recognition will come Milligan's way. Until then, perhaps, Mercy Flights will be his only monument.

6

Nate Saint of God's Kingdom of Flying Men

Nate Saint died along with four missionary companions. Their bodies were pierced by needle-sharp nine-foot hardwood spears. The most savage Stone Age Tribe left on Earth had triumphed—tentatively.

The crystal on Nate Saint's wristwatch was smashed and the hands stopped moving at 3:12 (P.M.) as the muddy waters of the Curaray River seeped into the broken case.

What the Auca Indians, deep in the tangled jungles of Ecuador, were not aware of on that fateful January day in 1956 was that men with burning zeal had, through the centuries, been triumphant in death in the spreading of Christianity.

Nate's crusade to spread Christianity had its beginning at age 13. Stricken with osteomyelitis and fearing the worst, he promised God that "if He would let me live, my life would henceforth belong to HIM."

Even then airplanes were his passion. Drawings of airplanes adorned his schoolbooks. He built and flew gliders. While still in his teens he earned money for flying lessons. Despite a pilot rating, he was turned down for flying cadet training. He spent the World War II years as a mechanic with the Army Air Force. Thereafter he entered Wheaton College in Illinois to prepare himself for foreign-mission service. Inwardly there were regrets his flying days were probably over.

Because "opportunity" has a way of tripping

NATE SAINT: GOD'S KINGDOM OF FLYING MEN • 123

up well-laid plans, so it was that there came a knocking—or rather a pounding—on Nate's door.

In California some ex-service pilots were putting together a missionary flying service. The Missionary Aviation Fellowship, as it was called, needed pilots with mechanical skill and religious fervor. To Nate, the news of MAF was the voice of God. He dropped his college course and hurried to Los Angeles.

The story of the Missionary Aviation Fellowship begins during the closing days of World War II. That was when Navy pilot Jim Truxton learned of the difficulties of missionaries cut off from civilization. Weeks, even months were sometimes spent slogging through jungles, climbing mountains, and traveling up rivers to reach their stations. Truxton reasoned that time and distance would be practically eliminated with a special air-service arm.

As he pondered the idea further he visualized airlift stations established in remote but centralized locations. They would serve all missions, regardless of denomination, within flying reach. The missions would pay the cost of gas, oil, maintenance, insurance, and also contribute to a fund for the eventual replacement of the aircraft. The cost per station would be only a small part of the total cost involved.

Truxton concluded the pilots must have unusual technical abilities as well as skill in flying. This built-in requirement would eliminate costly maintenance crews, but moreover and importantly, the resulting high degree of personal confidence would largely offset the hazards of over-jungle flying.

In Los Angeles, Jim Truxton's infectious vision struck a responsive chord with Grady Parrott, ex-AAF flight instructor, Charles Mellis, ex-B-17 pilot, and Elizabeth Green, ex-WASP. It was these four who launched the non-profit worldwide service.

Eventually the MAF built a kingdom of youthful flying men, serving church missions in the jungles of South America, Asia and Africa. Their planes kept evangelical agencies supplied with food, medicine, odds-and-ends and mail. They also carried doctors to the sick and sick to the hospital. Once an airlift was established the service proved indispensable. However, at the time Nate Saint joined MAF it was in its infancy. He was asked to pioneer a program in Ecuador.

Nate, with his brand new wife, Marjorie, flying a Stinson Voyager, arrived in Ecuador in the latter part of 1948. His assignment was an abandoned airstrip hacked out of the jungles by the Shell Oil Company. Shell Mera had served satellite camps in oil exploration. But when more blood flowed than oil—attacks from the savage Auca Indians—these outposts were abandoned. In the end the Shell project was terminated, thus making Shell Mera and other airstrips available for MAF activities.

An encouraging moment for Nate Saint pictured with an Auca feathered headband placed as an exchange gift during bucket drop.

Nate was to learn that the Auca Indians were so vicious that even the head-hunting Jivaros feared to enter their territory. Exactly where and how they lived was largely a mystery, for no one had penetrated the general area of Auca country and lived to tell the tale. What Nate heard was that these ferocious warriors went through the jungles as invisible wraiths, flinging their needle-sharp spears with deadly accuracy, spreading terror among the settlements of the various tribes.

Nate's immediate task was to establish a network of airstrips and a radio communication system with the missionary stations he would serve. Within months he transformed a way of life for the isolated stations. Radiophones kept all in daily touch. Moreover, instead of the missionaries spending days to walk in or out of the jungle, they now had instant plane transportation. Regular deliveries of mail, medicines and supplies were made in the Stinson Voyager, that is, until it was washed out at Quito.

The airstrip at Quito is at 9300 feet elevation and subject to tricky air currents off the surrounding mountains. On Nate's takeoff he was 200 feet into the air when caught in a violent down-draft. The ground impact broke off the engine and landing gear. Momentum bounced the wreckage into an upside-down flip. Nate sustained a back injury that kept him immobile for some time. When he began flying again it was in a new Piper Family Cruiser.

It was while Nate was recuperating that two further aircraft crashes gave him cause to ponder "the removal of the nerve-gnawing characteristics of our work." A Shell Grumman went down. Two lives lost. An Ecuadoran transport plane crashed. Eleven killed, no survivors. All of Nate's missions had been hazardous ones by American flying standards. An engine malfunction would likely be in the fuel system rather than in the dual ignition, he reasoned.

"I sit above the jungle listening for symptoms of trouble I never want to hear," Nate wrote to his brother, Sam, also a pilot. In the back of his mind, he knew someday, somehow, he would devise an alternate fuel system.

In the short months in Ecuador, Nate had on more than one occasion demonstrated a talent for ingenious handiwork. The wives of the missionaries living in primitive conditions welcomed his household gadgets and improvising, and in Nate's home it was Rube Goldberg devices that lightened Marjorie's daily chores.

The desperate need for developing an alternate fuel system was prompted by Bob Hart's grim experience. Hart, a pilot of the Gospel Missionary Union, was flying with George Poole, a pilot friend, over the jungles when the engine started cutting out and cutting in, in spite of all valiant efforts with cockpit valves and switches. Between cuts the engine would build back up to full power. Each burst of power brought new hope. But with each passing minute and mile, the declining needle on the altimeter and the descent toward treetops steadily revealed what was inevitable. Before the crash the engine picked up with enough power to clear a giant tree directly in their path. On the stall-out the plane dropped through a curtain of jungle to land upside down.

Both men survived the crash, but Hart's ankle and knee were broken. Poole, without serious injuries, struck out for civilization. Not until eleven days later was Hart rescued by missionary Dave Cooper and Indians assisting in the search.

The time had come for Nate Saint to develop an alternate fuel system.

Experimenting with the engine running, Nate lifted the cowling of the Piper, removed the temperature gauge fitting from the intake manifold, and squirted in gasoline. Each squeeze of a gas-loaded tube brought a burst of power. Encouraged, Nate borrowed one of Marjorie's cooking-oil cans for use as an auxiliary tank and fixed it to the struts of the left wing. To provide a streamline fairing, a piece of balsa wood was whittled into proper shape and attached. Salvaged fittings, strainer, and a screw-type valve made up the assembly. The valve was mounted on the fire wall with a control rod extended to the instrument panel. When completed, Nate took the Piper up for a test.

"Two thousand feet above the landing strip I pulled the mixture to idle-cutoff," he wrote. "It was quite a novel experience for a fellow who had listened so long, hoping never to hear it happen. But a turn of the little T-handle on the instrument panel brought with it a wonderful feeling as the engine wound back up to smooth full power. It picked up from the windmilling condition without a cough."

In time the alternate fuel system was adopted for all MAF planes.

Not all flights were routine. Where a missionary was visiting villages far from an airstrip, Nate experimented with parachute drops. Too often, instead of hitting the sandbar in the river, shifting wind currents carried the loaded parachute to tops of trees, or to an inaccessible part of the jungle. When this occurred he would tell himself there had to be a better way. But no idea was forthcoming until one day when he was confronted with what appeared to be a real emergency.

As he flew over a village he was attracted by the Indians waving white cloths. When he circled for a better look he saw an Indian lying in the clearing with arms outstretched. Sick or wounded? He had no way of knowing. It would take a week for a runner to penetrate the jungle to the nearest station. After dropping aspirins, Nate flew home with his mind seeking a solution to the problem that had perplexed him for some time.

And like many great ideas that spring from small, obscure beginnings, so did the solution come to him full-bloom as the Piper cruised above the deceiving, solid matting of jungle.

His mind went back to a day at Wheaton College. As the professor droned on at the blackboard, Nate, for lack of attention, occupied himself by idly swinging a string in a circle to which a pencil was attached at the lower end. He observed a curious thing. Although he increased the diameter of circular motions he was making with his hand, the pencil dangling beneath remained relatively stationary. He filed away the seemingly unimportant incident in his memory bank and forgot about it, until—

Over the jungles of Ecuador the memory bank, in a computer-like manner, sorted out a million filed-away incidents to produce this one recollection.

Would the same principle work if an object to be delivered were to be lowered on a line from a plane circling overhead? To test his assumptions he began experimenting with a canvas bucket attached to a stout fish line.

Afterwards Nate set down his findings.

"I circled at 1000 feet with the bucket trailing some 1500 feet behind. I banked and turned sharply, gradually making the circle smaller. Up until now the bucket had traveled at 60 miles per hour. Now it began to move slowly. The large arc of cord behind it bent toward the center of the circle, permitting the bucket to settle downward toward the point of a huge, invisible cone. Finally it came to rest in the field."

The first real test of the Nate Saint bucket drop came shortly later. Frank Mathis of Wycliffe Bible Translators had received an urgent call for help from the Arapicos Indians, and was heading for their village when Nate received additional word that the village was contaminated with a highly contagious disease. One victim had died.

Nate had in the meantime improved the bucket drop system by using 1500 feet of wire and including a telephone in the bucket. On the flight to the Arapicos village, missionary Bob Hart accompanied him. Over the village they spotted Mathis. Unreeling the wire and phone within a bucket, Nate succeeded in setting it in the center of the village.

"Hello, Frank," Nate's passenger began, speaking into the plane's phone. "This is Bob Hart."

"Bob, we've got a bad situation here," explained Mathis. "About half the village is down with stomach aches, headaches, leg cramps, cold extremities and clenched teeth."

"Stand by while we get in touch with the doctor in Quito."

In a matter of minutes, while Nate continued circling, holding the bucket just off the ground, Hart got in touch with the doctor over the Piper's short-wave radiophone. On hearing the symptoms and advising that Mathis was in no danger, the doctor, talking from 200 miles away, prescribed the necessary medicine.

The use of the convenient bucket drop became rather commonplace. It is ironic that Nate's inventive handiwork was to set in motion a chain of events leading to his death.

The project that involved five youthful missionaries was dubbed by them "Operation Auca." Its beginning occurred on the brilliantly clear day of September 19, 1955. As Nate took off on an emergency flight for Arajuno he noted the unusual clearness of the sky. Visibility, normally much limited by haze, was at least 75 miles. It would be an ideal day to carry on the continuing search for Auca villages.

After sitting down on the pencil-thin slash with dense jungle pressing on both sides of the Arajuno airstrip, Nate delivered to Ed McCully, the station missionary, the needed injection syringe to treat a sick Quechua Indian. Then he addressed him with, "It's so clear today, and I've got a little time, how about us going to look for the 'neighbors'?" The Aucas were always spoken of as "neighbors."

Ed, as usual, was receptive to the idea. "I say, Nate, you're reading my mind."

They first flew eastward 50 miles, then north toward the river Napo, all the while with faces pressed against the plexiglass. They saw nothing except endless miles of jungle, until they reached a point where the gas was getting low and they would have to direct their course to Arajuno. It was then that Nate unexpectedly caught sight of a clearing, not large, actually little more than enough to provide space for a house. He circled the area, and to their amazement they counted fifteen more such clearings and houses. After hundreds of flights in search of the Aucas, the discovery of the village—no natives were seen—left the two explorers breathless with elation.

From that moment on began the countdown. Nate and Ed, and those who would join the venture, had only three months and twenty days to live.

The time had come to share their discovery with Jim Elliott, whose station was at Shandia, and Peter Fleming at Puyu Pungu. Later, Roger Youderian would be included. The one thing all the young missionaries had in common was that in college each had been a campus leader. All were in their twenties except Nate, the old man of 31.

The plan of Operation Auca was to first soften up Auca hostility with a long and cautious campaign of airborne friendliness. Regular weekly flights would be made over the villages (on subsequent flights others were discovered). By bucket drops gifts would be left. However, there was the one perplexing question: Would the Aucas approach the bucket to remove the gifts? Assuming they wouldn't—at first, at least—Nate, with characteristic inventiveness, designed a release mechanism. It was of simple solution, involving two loops of wire held together by a hook. The hook was held in place by the weight of a broom handle attached to the hook. When the broom handle touched ground, the hook fell clear and the bucket tied to the lower loop was detached from the line.

The next morning Ed and Nate, brimming with anticipation, delivered the first gift. It was an aluminum kettle with bright-colored streamers attached, in which were placed colored buttons and a bag of salt.

Fortunately for posterity, Nate Saint was a prolific writer. His letters, reports, notes and journals, if published, would fill volumes. There are 39 pages of his unfinished account of Operation Auca. Regarding the first drop, he wrote:

> We continued circling until the gift was drifting in a small lazy circle below us, ribbons fluttering nicely. Finally the gift appeared to be pretty close to the trees below. Once I believe the ribbons dragged across a tree and hung up momentarily. We held our breath while the kettle lowered toward the earth. It hit about two or three feet from the water directly in line with the path to the house. Finally the line was free and there was our messenger of good will, love and faith two thousand feet below on the sandbar. In a sense we had delivered the first gospel message by sign language to a people a quarter of a mile away vertically, fifty miles horizontally, and continents and wide seas away psychologically.

They saw no Aucas, but on the second trip a week later, they noted the kettle was gone. Moving farther upstream where four canoes were beached before a big leaf house, Nate and Ed lowered a machete and for the first time were seeing the Aucas. Seemingly unafraid, a half-dozen or so naked Indians watched the dangling gift as it came lower to fall into the stream. Instantly it was retrieved to be examined by all.

In the weeks ahead, the flights brought about a rapport of sorts with the Aucas. Soon they were converging on the bucket drops with obvious delight. In what was accepted as a gesture of friendship, the Aucas attempted to match the missionaries' bounty. They in turn placed gifts in the bucket. Food. Comb. Headband. Live parrots. Operation Auca was making progress faster than anticipated.

Encouraged by gestures of friendly waving, the two missionaries decided the time had come to establish a beachhead in Auca-land. And so, early in December, Ed and Nate, together with Jim Elliott and Peter Fleming, began making plans. They agreed that every consideration, including the weather, seemed to be catapulting them toward their D-Day with a now-or-never exigency. Within a month the rainy season would start, flooding the rivers and making landings impossible. In the first week of January there would be a full moon. Accordingly, the date set was for January 3, 1956. While preparations were being made, Roger Youderian joined Operation Auca.

The only possible landing sites were sandbars on the Curaray River.

After considerable exploration Nate found a

likely sandbar some four miles from a village. But there were doubts if the sandbar offered sufficient length for takeoff. A determination would have to be made before an initial landing.

The flying missionary solved the problem in his own ingenious way. Experimenting at Shell Mera, he perfected a unique method—so simple, yet who other than Nate Saint would have thought of it?

Into one-pound paper sacks he placed yellow paint pigment powder. These were dropped from the Piper Cruiser, while flying at precisely 65 miles per hour, and at intervals of seven seconds. The bags split on landing, scattering the bright pigment and consistently marked off a space of approximately 200 yards. This length was deemed sufficient to get the Piper off a sandbar. Returning to the river, Nate, on dropping the yellow pigments, found the sandbar to be the space of two markers.

Ed McCully's Arajuno station was within 15 minutes' flying time of the Curarary River beachhead, so for the venture it became the staging area. Here the wives gathered with their husbands during the last-minute preparations. Check lists and flying schedules were made. Supplies of food, equipment, an aluminum prefabricated tree house, and gifts for the Aucas were arranged in priority piles. On the eve of D-Day, the wives and husbands soberly reassessed the risks for the last time. Did the young wives intuitively sense what lay ahead? Perhaps. In any case they were ready,

NATE SAINT: GOD'S KINGDOM OF FLYING MEN • 137

as were their husbands.

On the following morning at 8:02, only two minutes behind schedule, Nate and Ed took to the air. A few minutes later they were making a hazardous landing on the sandbar. Ed remained, while Nate began ferrying men and supplies. First on the agenda was the tree house. It was placed high enough to avoid spears. Although the missionaries worked in haste, no Aucas came to disturb them. But were they being watched? Likely so, if the strange bird calls from within the jungle meant anything—such as being man-made.

On Wednesday, the second day, the jungle was suspiciously silent. The day passed slowly. The missionaries, when not attending to camp duties, spaced themselves along the beach. Here they shouted Indian phrases of welcome and waved gifts. No Aucas presented themselves, nor did they on Thursday. That evening Nate wrote in his diary, "It is no small thing to try to bridge the twentieth century and the Stone Age."

Friday. January 6. Sometime during mid-morning the missionaries were suddenly struck dumb on seeing a man and woman, each about 30 years of age, step from the jungle on the other side of the river. They were followed by a well-formed girl of about 16. In the fashion of the jungle, they wore only the vine G-string.

The Auca man began speaking in a torrent of non-stop shouting, and at the same time pushing the girl forward in gestures that clearly suggested she was being offered for pagan love or trade.

"They've come," Jim Elliott yelled as he splashed across the shallow river.

The girl came forward to stand on a log at the water's edge. By the time Jim reached the opposite bank, the man and woman had joined the girl. Jim seized their hands and led them across. In camp whatever uneasiness the Indians may have had was soon dispelled with gifts of paring knives and the marvels of rubber bands, balloons, and the yo-yo. Again it was made quite clear the girl had been offered as a gift, and during her stay she appeared to be most disappointed that the men were not fulfilling the role expected. Over a beachfire hamburgers were cooked and served with mustard. These the Indians ate with the same impassiveness as looking at pictures in a *Time* magazine. But the man and girl did show an interest in the Piper. In fact, the man, by sign language, indicated a desire to be given a ride. When Nate agreed, he eagerly climbed in and strangely showed no fear. Over his village he waved and shouted to those below who recognized him with open mouths.

The balance of the day was spent attempting to get further acquainted with the Aucas, making a photographic record, and by sign language suggesting an invitation to their village. As time passed the girl showed a growing tendency toward impatience. She finally wandered off. The man called after her, then followed. Later the woman left.

Understandably, the missionaries were overjoyed. Months of preparation and years of dreaming had brought them face to face with the savage "neighbors." They were the first white men to ever do so on a friendly basis. In high spirits Nate and Peter flew to Arajuno to relate the wonderful experience to the waiting wives.

The next day, Saturday, was somewhat anticlimactic. Although the missionaries waited hopefully, no Aucas came. On the first flight over the village, Nate was puzzled to see the women and children run for cover. On a later flight he dropped gifts and there were some displays of friendliness, but not the exuberance of the past. Was the Indians' behavior an omen of impending misfortune, to read and be guided accordingly? If so, it was largely ignored.

Sunday. Promptly at 12:35 P.M., Nate Saint began his last radiophone conversation with his wife. He told her he had just flown over the village and returned. The village was practically deserted, but returning he spotted ten Aucas following the riverbank toward their beachhead camp. He finished his talk on a note of optimism. "Looks like they'll be here for an early afternoon service. Pray for us. This is the day! Will contact you next at 4:35."

The contact was never made because the lifeblood of the five missionaries had poured out shortly after three o'clock.

(Above) The Auca does not appear savage when introduced to a model airplane and an American hamburger, yet later he returned with others to murder the five missionaries.

(Below) The negative in Nate Saint's camera retrieved from the river, featured the two Auca women.

NATE SAINT: GOD'S KINGDOM OF FLYING MEN • 141

For the waiting wives the hours dragged by. In the seven years of jungle flying, Nate had never missed a prearranged radio call. Faithfully the wives waited at the radio transmitter, but not a crackle broke the silence. And as the hours and minutes passed they clung to each little hope, refusing to believe the worst could have happened.

Monday. At 7:00 A.M. Johnny Keenan, at Marjorie Saint's request, was flying toward the sandstrip Nate had previously pointed out to him. He too was an MAF pilot.

At 9:30 his call came through. He had seen the Piper. The fabric was stripped off. But on circling he saw no bodies, which for the moment gave some faint hope. However, on successive flights that day, he began seeing bodies downstream in the water. And with these reports all hope vanished.

Fellow missionaries, friendly Quechua Indians, American Air Force personnel and planes from Panama, a detachment of Ecuadorian soldiers with helicopter, all mounted a coordinated search operation by air and boats. They found the stripped Piper as reported, a rifled camp, and four spear-pierced bodies floating face downward. Ed McCully's body was seen and identified by Quechua Indians who arrived ahead of the main search party. But in the meantime it disappeared beneath the muddy waters and was never found. Nate Saint's body appeared to have been singled out for special vengeance, for the hardwood spear that pierced his body had attached to it pages of a Gospel tract believed to have been included in a bucket drop.

At the wishes of the wives the four missionaries were buried on the beach in one grave. They were buried under the tree house that was to have served as a refuge in the event of an attack. "It's the most beautiful cemetery in the world," observed Marjorie Saint when she saw the lonely mound from the air.

Mostly the world accepted the deaths as an enormous waste of life. But it was Ed McCully's father who put a different perspective on the tragedies. He said, "God makes no mistakes."

And so it would seem today, for the wives of the slain missionaries, staying on in missionary work, saw within a few years Christianity being accepted by the Aucas. The first acceptance was by women fleeing the tribe, later by men and women as a result of the MAF's extensive crusade to convert the people from cruel and wanton savagery through Christian teachings.

Time, the measurer of all things, will surely accord Nate Saint with lasting greatness. Certainly he will be remembered for the Christian work that accelerated with his death, for his jungle-flying techniques, and for the bringing of greater reliability to aircraft engines. And measuring all these accomplishments, did he not abundantly fulfill the promise he made as a boy of 13? It would seem so.

7

A Hayfield for Takeoffs

The engine of the red Monocoupe caught as the pilot, with little effort, gave a downward swing of the propeller. Then the engine picked up with a steady rhythm, making little vibrations dance through the plane. Through the plexiglass a boy in the left-hand seat saw the pilot circle the blur of propeller, duck under the wing, and come to the open door of the cockpit.

"I'm going to pull the wheel chocks," the pilot said, reaching inside and easing back on the throttle. "Hold back the stick . . . that's right, all the way back."

It was a simple thing, the holding back of the stick, pressing it into his lap and feeling the air pressures of the elevator surfaces pushing the tail down. For Duane Cole—unknowingly, of course—it was a significant moment. This was the beginning of a lifetime career in aviation. More specifically, a lifetime devoted to barnstorming, airshows and aerobatics. The end result would be his name known in practically every hangar in the world. However, at that moment Duane's thoughts were hardly on a nebulous future.

Instead he was wondering why he was spending the last of his money for a bit of air instruction. Was he out of his mind? On this unhappy Christmas Day in the pre-World War II years, when the country was paralyzed by the Great Depression, you had to be out of your mind to spend your last cent for something you couldn't eat. And yet he was doing it in a sort of mad abandonment from reality.

Why—?

Without actually analyzing it, the answer was there in the back of his mind. A whole complex set of circumstances led him from his home to Phoenix, Arizona, to the Sky Harbor Airport, and into this now gently throbbing airplane.

Before the dreadful "Black Friday" in Illinois when scores of banks closed their doors, and before corn dropped from one dollar a bushel to nine cents, the Rolla Cole family of nine boys and one daughter had never known real want. Their 240-acre farm on Indian Creek at Toulon had provided a mortgage base to invest in California properties. People with money were either investing in stocks and bonds or else in further property. Good times begat good times was the universal concept. At first the depression clouds were faint on the horizon. As times got worse people were saying, "Things can't go on like this." They were right in a sense. Conditions went from bad to the inconceivable. Millions of supposedly substantial families were reduced to direst poverty. Included was the Cole family.

After losing their farm the small, four-room tenant house provided by a charitable farmer, while appreciated, contributed to an agonizing stigma to be suffered in silence. As the days slipped by, frustrations deepened with the lack of elbow room, the lack of work, and having meal after meal of mostly potatoes. To ease the strain, to "get away from it all," the older boys left home. One by one they left, to hitchhike the Big Road without definite aims except to seek work, any kind of work that would maintain respect.

Duane's wanderings took him across the country to the Northwest with a pause at Dorris, California. Here he became—of all things—a cowboy. For five months he rode the range. When he left the rancher gave him $20. It was all he could spare for Duane's summer work.

Following the Big Road with his thumb, Duane discovered a five-cent can opener was a wonderful investment. It would open a ten-cent can of beans. With a loaf of stale bread—usually for the asking—one had a nourishing meal. He found too that carrying a suitcase, keeping his shoes polished, avoiding the grime of freight trains and hobo jungles, jobs had an unexpected way of turning up, although the pay might be only a dollar a day. During these wanderings Duane often found solace from despair at airports. An engine warming up, a plane taking off, somehow eased the burden of his mind. In time he drifted to Phoenix, Arizona. A couple of jobs and promise of others held him there, largely because a kindly landlady told him he could pay her "when he got the money." Eventually he did, in an unexpected way.

When he saw others making application for Christmas work at the post office, he too filled out an application, although he had small hope of being accepted. The interview that followed was brief, four or five minutes at most. When he was told, "Come back tomorrow," it took several seconds for the implication to sink in. In the days ahead he sorted a million letters, more or less, putting them in little pigeonholes in a case before him.

It was this timely manna from Uncle Sam that paid the landlady, bought a few needed clothes, and made a somewhat brighter Christmas at home. He had the choice of buying less or no clothes or of sending a smaller package home, but he followed none of these choices and consequently he was left with only one dollar and a half on Christmas morning.

Although there was satisfaction of being "square with the world," the feeling, however, did not compensate for being away from home. The indelible memories of happier Christmases with the family gathered around the tree, when excited kids unwrapped presents, gave him pangs of homesickness he had never known before. In the past, to ease homesickness, he had taken long walks. While these walks were usually started without purpose or direction, they almost always ended at the local airport. This time Duane went directly to the Sky Harbor Airport.

It was a cloudless morning, no wind, and the sun was pleasantly warm. It surprised Duane to find no flying activity. Actually, the airport looked deserted. But when he looked closer, he saw a man slouched in a chair outside a hangar office. Before Duane was close enough to exchange a "Merry Christmas," he noted the FLY TODAY sign had its $3 crossed out and $2 in newer paint.

The man was perhaps in his late thirties and wore what most pilots were wearing—baggy golf knickers and leather jacket. Among the flying fraternity this garb had come to replace boots and whipcord breeches and the white scarfs of barnstorming days. After the exchange of Christmas greetings, Duane was conscious of the other taking his measure.

The man was seeing a slender boy in his late teens with the stamp of a high school athlete, if the letterman's T on his sweater meant anything.

"Football?"

"Football and basketball," Duane told him. One thing about the T, it was a never-fail gimmick for opening conversations. And the T, perhaps as much as anything, had opened doors of opportunity, at least enough for Duane to get his feet in. It had gotten him rides to other cities and jobs that otherwise would never have materialized. In short, the T had helped him recover from more than one blind-side tackle the Big Road dealt him.

"Tonopah?"

Duane shook his head. "No, the T stands for Toulon . . . Toulon, Illinois."

"Illinois—. I learned to fly at Chanute Field. 1917. . . Where's Toulon?"

"In Stark County . . . between Peoria and Rock

Island."

The pilot stretched lazily in the chair. "Never got that far north. But I'll tell you one thing, there's no place like Illinois to fly. The country is flat enough to sit down anywhere. All the fence lines run north-and-south, and east-and-west. You don't really need a compass."

This was as far as the small talk got, for the office phone rang. The pilot bolted from the chair. Duane heard him say, "It's pretty dead out here..." Without waiting to hear more he angled over to a Velie Monocoupe on the hangar apron.

The cockpit, Duane saw, was fitted with dual controls. Through the plexiglass windscreen he saw the pilot come to the doorway and stand looking his way. And Duane knew that as sure as God made little green apples he was going to be asked to fly. It came almost instantly.

"How about a hop? Give you a long ride for two bucks."

Duane's grin was as friendly as a shaggy dog edging up for a pat on the head. He answered, "Haven't got two dollars."

The pilot came back real fast, "Maybe you got one-fifty?"

Duane hesitated, then admitted, "Guess I got that much. But I can't afford it."

The pilot glanced up at the sky, as if from habit, then moved out of the doorway. He walked over to Duane unhurriedly, as if trying to show disinterest, but under the surface there was faint restraint.

At first the pilot's conversation avoided selling an airplane ride. He steered the talk from nice day to times are tough to Roosevelt is ruining the country. At length he maneuvered the conversation back to flying and after relating a few anecdotes, he came right out and asked, "Why don't you give yourself a Christmas present? I'll tell you what I'll do. It being Christmas, I'll shave the price fifty cents, and give you the same amount of time in the air."

"Will you give me a flying lesson for one dollar and fifty cents?" The words popped out spontaneously. Now that he had said it, he knew he wanted to go through with the deal if the pilot was willing.

The pilot's eyes narrowed. His opening gambit hadn't gone the expected way.

"Suppose I give you a short lesson at that price. What's the chances of my giving more lessons—not at a cut rate, mind you, but at a regular price?"

Duane shook his head. He told enough to reveal the hopelessness of making promises. Then in a few stumbling words he got across that what he wanted more than anything else was to be a pilot. That said, he rested his case.

For a long moment the pilot looked at the boy before him. He did not try to put his thoughts into words, but it was plain to see he was thinking. Maybe he was remembering that he was once a boy wanting more than anything else to be a pilot. Anyway, after the long pause he said abruptly, "Get into the plane. I don't know whether I'm doing a dumb thing or not, but you're going to get a half hour of instruction with no corners cut."

While strapping Duane in he kept on talking as if more to himself than to Duane. "I've done some dumb things in my life, I'll admit. And some of the dumb things I've done have turned out to be not so dumb after all..."

It was late spring when Duane returned home with some three hours of instruction to his credit. Times were getting better now. The country was slowly crawling out of the depression. When a factory in Peoria began hiring, sixteen-year-old brother Lester dropped out of school to support the family with a man-sized job. Duane was hired on shortly after. Although the brothers shared their paychecks at home, Duane managed to fly some at the Peoria Mt. Hawley Airport. With an eye on a future in the sky, Duane reasoned that with a Cub plane he could build up flying time at little cost. His enthusiasm infected Lester. Together they bought a 37-hp Taylorcraft. The down payment was made by mortgaging a sow and pigs. To keep their father occupied, the older brothers had managed to send enough money home to buy a cow, pigs and poultry. Duane's contribution was the pigs.

With a little time in the air, Duane got the idea

of barnstorming.

"Barnstorming," snorted an old-timer at the Peoria airport. "Listen, Duane, barnstorming went out with flagpole sitting. Don't you know airplanes ain't a novelty anymore, and people don't have money for rides, and besides..."

With the sour words of an expert ringing in their ears, Duane and Lester flew to Lafayette the following Sunday. Landing in a hayfield, they soon attracted farmers and townspeople. At two dollars a hop the Taylorcraft was kept busy until gathering dusk made it necessary to fly back to Peoria. Thereafter on weekends for the next year or so, Duane and Lester (Lester in the meantime had learned to fly) flew off central Illinois cow pastures and hayfields. Sometimes, with the use of two Taylorcrafts, they made as much as $100 a day—a month's wages at the factory.

In 1940 the Depression abruptly ended. War clouds on the horizon stirred the War Department to hastily build training camps. Industry geared to a possible onslaught. The tempo of the country accelerated in a drive for preparedness. Duane aided in the get-ready-for-war effort by teaching flying in a college flight program at Waterman. With his afternoons and evenings free, he took over management of nearby Streetor Airport. Marion, the youngest brother and barely sixteen, joined him as hangar boy. And thereby hangs a tale legends are made of.

Marion taught himself to fly in a J3 Cub during

Duane's morning absences. With less than two hours of dual instruction, he, with his self-instruction, successfully soloed! Moreover, like a kid caught with his hand in the cookie jar, he was seen circling the airport by big brother Duane, who incidentally was returning from Waterman earlier than expected.

Duane met the serious infraction in a sensible way. When Marion taxiied to the hangar and climbed out of the cockpit with a sheepish look, Duane told him, "I'm not going to let you kill yourself. Beginning right now you start taking flying lessons from me."

With the international situation deteriorating day by day President Roosevelt, in a vigorous, bold and far-seeing gesture, called for civilian pilots to train military pilots for an air power that eventually reached the staggering total of 2,500,000 men and 75,000 aircraft.

A tribute is due those civilian pilot instructors. During the depression the raggedy-pants flyers kept aviation alive. It took dedicated courage to spend precious dollars for flying when jobs and money were practically nonexistent. But in the hour of need, when the United States was suddenly caught between the hard rock and Hitler and Tojo's air might, thank our stars of destiny there were these pilots available to train a vast number for the military. The Cole brothers, Duane and Lester and Marion, became flight instructors in the war program.

The Cole Brothers during the war years. (top) Lester, (lower left) Duane, and (right) Marion.

Duane did a stint of teaching English cadets at Parker, Arizona, then joined Lester at War Eagle Field, Lancaster, California, teaching young Americans. Not until Marion reached 18 would he instruct for the Navy at Bloomington, Illinois. But before that, he surreptitiously taught flying at an Illinois airport, and thereby hangs another tale.

A well-known airport operator had weathered the lean years of the depression only to see his business in jeopardy when ailing health kept him immobile. So with the country drained of licensed instructors, he made use of Marion. Later, when Marion reached 18, he qualified for his commercial and instructor's rating on the day of his birthday. The next day he offered his services to the Navy.

In 1945 the struggle for victory moved swiftly to a climax as U.S. bombers broke the back of Germany and gave a knockout blow to Japan. Suddenly there was no more war. It was a glorious feeling. The country went wild. Several million servicemen were free to make dreams come true. Duane, Lester and Marion were not without dreams. Theirs would be a joint airport operation. They leased a hayfield bordering the town of Kewanee, Illinois.

To make themselves known, they put on an airshow. One of the attractions was "Colonel Joe Jet and His Fighting Wingmen." The crowd failed to appreciate the act when a lone Cub appeared and three guinea hens spiraled down to a neighboring barnyard. There was grumbling over false advertisement. The crowd's good humor returned with Duane hurriedly staging a "pants race" for fly-in pilots. It was a six-mile race around a pylon course. At the end of the first lap the pilots were to land and remove their pants on the far side of the runway, then continue another lap, land and put their pants on for a final lap. But on the second landing the pilots discovered their pants tied in knots and tossed in a pile in front of the crowd.

When the crowd roared at the antics of the chagrined pilots, a grey-bearded farmer dressed in traditional bib overalls and well-seasoned straw hat drove a farm tractor onto the field. Much to the apparent annoyance of pilots and officials and despite arguments, he left it sitting to amble among the planes kicking tires and behaving in the manner of a typical country rube. While a Cub was warming up he jumped into the cockpit, took off in an erratic manner and began clowning in the sky. The farmer—Marion Cole—wound up his performance by buzzing the freeloaders on the road, to the delight of the paid onlookers. But one of the outsiders let fly a rock. It scored a direct hit. A wing strut was caved in so badly Marion had difficulty landing back on the field.

It was from this badly arranged exhibition that the Cole Brothers Air Show was born. It was an opportune time, too, for this was the threshold of the Golden Age of airshows, the years 1946 to

1950. Aerial might had pretty much decided the war; consequently the public had a built-in acceptance of aerial displays. The availability of surplus Stearmans at low cost prompted a spate of airshow troupes.

Despite the competition, the Cole Brothers Air Show grew in stature. Theirs was a full-fledged traveling troupe with three Stearmans, a Great Lakes and a clipped wing Cub. The additional pilots, parachutists and wing riders were young friends. Arnold, another brother, joined the show as announcer.

One writer of the times captured the drama of smoke and noise. "Picture, if you will, a Cole Brothers Air Show opening scene. A hot, midwestern sun beats down on a Sunday airport crowd strung along a makeshift rope barrier. As one, all eyes are zeroed on three approaching Stearmans, gaudy in glistening colors, flying wing-to-wing above the runway. On they come, the white-clad wing riders with arms stretched birdlike. The raucous 'blat' of the 450 Pratt & Whitneys outracing the planes. As if on signal, silver smoke spews from each machine moments before the formation arches up in precision flying. With quickened pulses and necks craned, the crowd stares open-mouthed as the planes, invisibly linked, climb upward and ease over in perfect loops. Leaving graceful patterns of smoke, the trio scream down to level out before the spectators. A freckled boy, crowding the rope, bubbled with excitement. 'Wow,' he shouts above the din of snarling engines. A happy grin spreads across his face. In his own way he was expressing the sentiments of the crowd."

It was a glorious era. The cash register had a happy ring. The aura of electrified crowds seemed to the country boys a fulfillment of dreams. There is a uniqueness about brother participation, consequently reporters and magazine writers publicized the show with colorful copy. Their fame spread, especially after Marion won the National Aerobatic Championship at Miami and Lester was a high point winner.

In the early 1950s the glorious era began fading. With the passing years World War II was becoming more and more history and less reality. When attentions shifted to rockets and guided missiles, the airshows suffered accordingly. Duane met the decline by streamlining the troupe, eliminating additional pilots and planes, and using one wing rider instead of three. The adjustment was marginal, enough to stave off a possible end. Many airshows folded. Pickup groups provided cut-throat competition. What hurt most were the fast-buck promoters. They promoted shows by loudly proclaiming phony championship records for their pilots. Usually they failed to live up to contract agreements and were adept at conning gate receipts.

Another serious matter was airshows without

proper policing. Irresponsible practices went unchecked by "hot pilots" emulating Hollywood stunts of the 1920s. Never once did Duane permit stunting. All performances were precision aerobatics. What he feared most from the competition happened at Flagler, Colorado. There a HP-pilot came boring towards the crowd, trailing smoke. He zoomed up, stalled, and fell into the mass of spectators. He killed himself. Nineteen others died. Fifty were injured. Almost no family of the town's 793 population was left untouched by the tragedy. The Civil Aeronautics Administration reacted to the senseless deaths. Airshows were banned.

In his characteristic way of meeting challenges head on, Duane flew to Chicago to lay his case before the CAA regional manager.

"Duane, you know I can't make decisions here," Bill Wagner told him.

A phone call to administrator Fred Lee in Washington gave Duane hopes.

"I'm sure we can lift the ban, providing adequate policies and regulations are formulated," Lee told Duane. "Say, why don't you and Bill Wagner get in a huddle and work out something?"

Three days later the regional office turned in a draft that was largely the work of Duane. He had merely put down the safety practices long used by the Cole Brothers Air Show. Perhaps it is not too surprising the draft was adopted *in toto*. Shortly

(Above) The Cole Brothers' fame was spreading in 1949, when (l to r) Marion, Arnold, Lester and Duane were pictured in May issue, *Flying*. (Below) Rolly: "He had an uncommon touch."

after, airshows were back in business with sane restrictions.

However, the Flagler tragedy and subsequent ban had an adverse effect on the public and sponsors alike. Now the Cole Brothers Air Show was faced with cancellations and slender gate receipts. Figuratively, they spun in at Humboldt, Tennessee. After paying expenses they had exactly $28 to divide.

Sadly, the brothers discussed their plight. "We've got to split up," was the verdict. A smaller show, accepting only guaranteed bookings, would survive. Duane would continue in the name of Cole Brothers Air Show.

The phase-out period extended over weeks, but in the end Lester left to instruct at Flabob Airport, Riverside, California. Later, when Duane moved his operations from Kewanee to Fort Wayne, Indiana, Lester rejoined the show. When pioneer pilot Jack Fry, now heading the Fry Corporation, heard Marion was footloose, he gave him a test pilot job of the Skylark. It was a revolutionary STOL under development at Fort Worth, Texas. Marion found it to be a "hairy go" to fly. With airshow adrenalin lingering in his blood, he generally joined Duane and Lester in the big holiday events.

Ever since the days of pusher-type biplanes, when pilots wore their checkered caps backward, there have been airshows on the American scene. Yet in all the years, few troupes endured more than a season or two. That the Cole Brothers Air Show endured is a tribute to Duane's tenacity and a solid reputation for ethics and reliability. While their fame was growing, Hollywood sent for them to make a series of TV pictures.

After some lean years in the 1950s times got better; in fact, Duane reached a stage where he could pick and choose his bookings. Working in his favor was a growing family steeped in airshow lore. In the early 1960s the family replaced all members of the troupe with the exception of a parachute jumper. Duane and his son Rolly did the aerobatic acts. Duane's petite wife, Judy, rode the wing. John, at the age of 15, was the announcer. Even little Karen made herself useful. Lester and Marion took jobs as executive pilots for industrial firms.

The Duane Coles were a close-knit family. A happy family. For 30 weeks out of the year they lived a hurried, hectic life, crisscrossing the United States, usually in a mad rush to maintain a tight schedule. However, in doing so they got to know America first-hand. Geography and scenes of history became more real when viewed from the air.

Among the aerobatic fraternity the word was, "Keep an eye on Rolly. He's going to be the greatest." In his teenage days he was developing an uncommon touch that made his aerobatics pure artistry to watch. But was he as good as his

A HAYFIELD FOR TAKEOFFS • 163

(Above) The brothers grow older. (L to R) Marion, Lester and Duane in 1968. (Below) Judy Cole,

dad? Not since Marion won the National Aerobatic Championship at Miami had there been an official competitive airmeet. It was the Experimental Aircraft Association that awakened interest with a competitive airmeet at Phoenix, Arizona, in 1962. Duane and Rolly and a dozen top aerobatic pilots, flying beautifully modified jobs, accepted the challenge.

It was a day of high tensions at the Deer Valley Airport. Conspicuously absent were those pilots with phony championship records. About his son, Duane had mixed feelings. He knew he would be the happiest man in the world if Rolly won; still, he would do his best to beat him, and others, too. One by one the pilots flew the established route. The judges' final decision was: Duane Cole, first place; Rod Jocelyn, second; Rolly Cole, third; and Harold Krier, fourth. When congratulations were offered Duane he responded, "Thanks, but the big winner is the sport itself."

Although Rolly's star was ascending, a commitment to the Air National Guard prevented him from participating in the World Aerobatic Competition at Budapest, Hungary, in 1963. Duane, Rod Jocelyn and Lindsey Parsons represented the United States. They might just as well have stayed home. The odds were stacked against them. They were judged by last-minute, revised rules giving complete favor to the Iron Curtain countries. Little wonder the Western countries made poor showings.

A HAYFIELD FOR TAKEOFFS • 165

Rolly, following his stint in the Air National Guard, came home determined to wrest the international championship from the Iron Curtain countries. He practiced continuously. Sadly his dream was cut short August 2, 1963. While practicing over an Illinois cornfield there was an instantaneous breakup of the Stearman engine. The resultant sudden stoppage produced an overload that tore the engine from its mount. The separation of engine and airplane brought on an overload on wing fittings and spar. The top wing folded back over the front cockpit. It trapped a friend who had gone along for the ride. In Rolly's effort to save the other he delayed his jump too long.

Duane was grief-stricken and immediately terminated the airshow after 17 years of participation. In a period of mourning he wrote *To A Pilot*, a tribute to Rolly. One poignant passage reads:

> Now there are no contracts to be signed or publicity material to be mailed, no hurrying from town to town and no clothes to be packed, no more sleeping in motels, or hot dogs and soda pop for Sunday dinner, no new scenery to marvel at or strange fascinating cities to savor.
>
> We will accustom ourselves to living as others do. We will wash the car or clean the garage on Saturday and go visiting Saturday night. We will have roast beef dinner with mashed potatoes and gravy on Sundays after church and sit home watching television on Sunday afternoons and

evenings. Our habits will change and possibly our personalities. But as we look to this quiet future, we will be forever thankful for an exciting past.

Since that tragic year, Duane has written seven books, all successful sellers. In 1964 he won the National Aerobatic Championship for the second time. Writing, teaching aerobatics, and appearing at major airmeets as a guest exhibitionist has been his busy life in the intervening years.

His book, *The Flying Coles*, ends on this note:

> In the past thirty-nine years I have ridden the winds, jousted with the elements, rolled and looped and cavorted about the sky for more than 20,000 hours. I have never been bored. I estimate I have made 10,000 flights, each one a new experience. Each a challenge. I am a fortunate man in that my vocation would have been my hobby under other circumstances. The phase of aviation I chose was not one in which to become rich. Yet, it has been most rewarding. Applause for an exhibition well flown, a sincere thank you from an aerobatic student, the pride of seeing a protege doing well, being a part of a great expanding movement, and the fellowship of one's peers cannot be measured by monetary standards. They add up to the satisfaction of accomplishment, a feeling of well-being, and a sense of belonging.

EPILOGUE
A Message to the Boys of America

When I was a boy World War I captured the headlines and dominated everyone's thoughts. I remember how the spirit of patriotism ran feverishly high. Our only media in those days were the newspapers, and each day they were eagerly read for the latest battle accounts. When I read the papers I looked first for stories of aerial combat. Eddie Rickenbacker and Frank Luke led the list of my heroes. While plowing corn—I began farm work at the age of ten—I would daydream I was gloriously blasting away at the tail of a Fokker. I know now other kids lived in pretty much the same dream worlds as I. And so, for perhaps a million American boys it was the beginning of a lifetime interest in aviation.

Following the war came an era of barnstorming. Whenever a plane—always a war surplus Jenny—dropped in on a neighboring cow pasture, we ditched school to hungrily watch the takeoffs and landings. My first ride was in a Jenny—not a barnstorming Jenny, but rather with Chanute Field army markings. It was with a lieutenant who occasionally flew to my hometown to visit his girlfriend. During these years—the 1920s—cow pastures became airports with only the addition of a windsock and hangar. They attracted boys who came to just "hang around." Talk to the gray-haired pilots of today, and the chances are they will tell of those boyhood visits when there were no chainlink fences to keep kids out.

In those days every pilot wore a flap-eared helmet and goggles and was a hero of sorts. And why not? Every flight in a sense was an adventure. There was a pioneering spirit that prevailed. I guess everybody was more or less conscious of history being made.

Few boys lived near airports. However, that did not deter their interest in aviation. They read. In those pre-TV days, they turned to books and magazines. Many famous men in aviation owe their careers to early readings. A classic example is Charles Lindbergh. He was a farmboy during World War I. In the years 1917-19 a series appeared in *Everybody's Magazine* entitled "Tam o' the Scoots." The stories written by Edgar Wallace featured a fictional ace. They stimulated young Lindbergh so much he resolved to become a pilot. Eventually he made the dream come true, and in turn became the world's greatest aviation hero.

In the late 1920s and during much of the 1930s America was paralyzed by the Great Depression. The bleakness of growing up was largely offset by creating dream worlds from stories in books and magazines—especially some 30 pulp magazines. Aviation's heritage owes much to those authors that inspired a generation of youngsters.

At least a hundred juvenile aviation books were written. Mostly they were series written around a boy hero. High on the popularity list was the Bill Bruce series written by Major Hap Arnold. Few readers realized that the future Four Star General of World War II fame was immortalizing his son, William Bruce, in the hero role. Today collectors are paying five dollars and up for copies of *Bill Bruce and the Pioneer Aviators* — *and the Flying Cadets* — *Becomes an Ace* — *on the Border Patrol* — *on Forest Patrol*, and —*in the Transcontinental Race*. While Frederic Nelson Litten wrote a dozen or so aviation books for boys, his most popular were *Rhodes of the Flying Cadets* — *of the 94th*, and — *of the Leathernecks*. Other series were the Billy Smith Ace series by Noel Sainsbury, Jr., Rex Lee series by Thomson Burtis, Bob Wakefield series by Blaine and Dupont Miller, Ted Scott series by Franklin W. Dixon, and the list goes on and on. Lewis E. Theiss should be mentioned for his air mail, smugglers and border patrol stories.

The flying pulps deserve a special niche in aviation history. For ten years the colorful aerial scenes featured on the magazine covers dominated the drugstore racks across the nation. Young readers, fortunate to have a dime from mowing lawns, became big spenders. After reading the flying pulp of their choice, perhaps two or three times, each in turn passed his copy on to another fan for the other's latest acquisition. In turn both copies were traded for others, and so on until all possible trades exhausted the neighborhood supply. Generally by that time the new issues were on the stands. This junior trading enterprise was carried on week after week in every neighborhood in the U.S.A. It is the magnitude of this interest that makes the flying pulps an institution.

"I learned to read by reading the flying pulps." These are the words of Gene Olson, author of 17 books for boys, including *The Tin Goose*. "I learned my ABCs in school, but it was the flying pulps that provided the interest."

"When I was a boy I devoured them and a group of us would trade them around," declared Colonel Grover Heiman, USAF-Ret. "It was those stories that zeroed me in on wanting to fly and led to a 27-year career in the Air Force." Eventually Heiman wrote two successful boys' books, *Jet Tanker* and *Jet Navigator*.

Heiman's boyhood interest explains why kids caught up in World War II had a built-in eagerness to serve in the Air Force. And when the Air Age accelerated after the war, these kids, now men, studied aeronautics, and took flying jobs, and design jobs, and maintenance work, anything to stay in aviation. In time a lot of them provided the leadership to make America first in the Space Age.

When the flying pulps faded and died in the early 1940s, young readers were not neglected. A dozen book series appeared during World War II written around updated heroes. Instead of aerial dogfights in Spads, Camels and SE-5s, the new crop of heroes fought in P-40s, and P-51s, and B-17s, and B-24s, or whatever plane would lend itself to the plot.

When the war ended, by some unexplained coincidence an era ended. After nearly 30 years of an abundance of aviation stories for boys, suddenly there were no more. Although some of the big-name pulp writers turned to juveniles, it seems rather strange that with a couple of exceptions they wrote nothing of aviation. Instead they turned to sports, hot rods, and various adventures. Among those best remembered are Joe Archibald, John Scott Douglas, and Robert Sidney Bowen.

In the 1950s, emerging authors were setting a pace with a quality of writing that far exceeded the best works of previous years. Authors Gene Olson, Robb White, Frank Bonham, Colonel Red Reeder, and in fact all juvenile writers, were carrying on the same theme of clean-cut boys following the rules of fair play, yet the stories were written without cliff-hanging melodrama. The boy heroes continued to meet challenges in an honorable manner, whether it be on the baseball diamond, or playing football, or having adventures on land or sea. Only in a few exceptions were the storylines centered around aviation. To give an example of how much young readers of the 1950s,

1960s and 1970s have been denied aviation stories, one must realize that normally about 500 juveniles (for all ages) are published yearly. By my survey, less than 50 flying stories have appeared in the past 30 years. That figures less than two books per year. What is lamentable is that only eight titles have survived in print.

Of non-fiction books for young readers, only a scant few were published.

Old-timers of my generation are concerned that the youth of America has lost sight of aviation heritage. If flying stories were once the catalyst, then we feel rightly so there should be a revival of books to stir the interest. After all, it is a truism that fictional interest leads to factual interest.

So what is the solution?

To begin with there must be a worthwhile incentive to attract top writers. Ernest Gann, Martin Caidin, General Robert Scott, to name a few. They, and others of that caliber, have the flying experiences and writing know-how to turn out top-notch stories. To attract them and others, what better motive than a meaningful annual award for the best flying story? The award should have a stature of the Newbery Award. A prestige award, sponsored by an institution of respect, such as The American Aviation Historical Society, would certainly encourage writers, publishers and librarians alike. In turn the boys of America—and let's not forget the girls—would be caught up in the romance of flying history. They would get to know the era of pusher planes, and tractor biplanes with tailskids, and learn of those valiant pioneers who followed Lindbergh in overseas flights. They would learn of America's aces beginning with Eddie Rickenbacker and Frank Luke, and later, Dick Bong and Joe Foss. Moreover, they would likely learn much about the whole spectrum of aviation, for there is enough background material for a thousand themes.

Young Americans of today need this inspiration of history for guidance. They need it just as we of my generation needed inspirational history back in the days of the horse and buggy. Then, as now, the wave of the future lies with the younger generation.

This is a brief message tacked onto the end of my book. An old adage states, "One candle may light a thousand." Well maybe, just maybe, this message will set in motion a chain of circumstances that in the end will work wonders. Maybe, because all things are possible, it will prove to be the catalyst for a revival of flying stories. If so, and everything works out all right, then a lot of gray-haired pilots are going to have comfort knowing that young readers are not losing sight of America's precious aviation heritage.

ABOUT THE AUTHOR

"In 1929 I traded a Model T Ford for six hours of flying instruction in an OX-5 Swallow at Clover Field, Santa Monica, California."

Aviation. History. Writing. These have been Martin Cole's main interests.

Following the war years as an engineer officer with the U.S. Army Air Force, Cole became associated with the State of California as a historian-curator. In 1968 he retired to travel and further his writings. Traveling has taken he and Mrs. Cole to forty countries. Over the years some fifty articles of his have appeared in national publications. He has written two regional books on Don Pio Pico, the last governor of Mexican California. Aside from these busy pursuits, Cole has served as a Director of the American Aviation Historical Society. For three years he was editor of its *Journal.* The Coles live in Whittier, California.

ABOUT THE ARTIST

Born in 1944, James H. Farmer has had a lifelong love affair with aviation, all of which has been manifested in aviation art, photography and writings. His art has appeared mainly in the JOURNAL published by the American Aviation Historical Society, and in 1977 he won the contributor's award for a cover painting of the P-47s of the 35th Fighter Group. Previously, in 1974, his manuscript, "The Making of Twelve O'Clock High," won the AAHS contributor's award. Some forty published articles have appeared in national publications. His photos have appeared in scores of aviation magazines, including the covers of international publications.

Mr. Farmer has had a long association with the American Aviation Historical Society, serving on the staff at various times as Associate Editor, and later Art Editor. He is currently a member of the Society's Board of Directors.

Aside from these activities, Farmer is a senior high school art and history instructor; moreover he is working on his first book of aviation history. The Farmers reside in Glendora, California.